Also available from Marshall Pickering
by the same author

The Torn Veil

Beyond the Veil

Sister Gulshan Esther

with Vita Toon

Marshall Pickering
An Imprint of HarperCollins*Publishers*

Marshall Pickering
An imprint of HarperCollins*Religious*
Part of HarperCollins*Publishers*
77–85 Fulham Palace Road,
Hammersmith, London W6 8JB

Published by Marshall Pickering 1992
9 8 7 6 5 4 3 2

A catalogue record for this book
is available at the British Library

Phototypeset by Input Typsetting Ltd, London
Printed in Great Britain by
HarperCollinsManufacturing Glasgow

For Susan,
whose devotion and care have to be
seen to be believed

Note to the Reader

Names of people and of some places have been changed to preserve anonymity

Contents

Chapter 1

To London

'Ma-ji, we shall miss you. Come back to us soon', echoed Zenith, Razia, Sheila and Edwin, my four adopted children, as we said goodbye to each other at the airport in Lahore. It was Saturday, 25th September 1982, and I was on my way to England with an overnight stop in Karachi. On arrival there, my friends Mr and Mrs Manny met me and took me to their home. A few friends had gathered to share this memorable evening with me. All night long we stayed up, praying, singing psalms and hymns, and reading from the Word of God. My friends were concerned for me because of my lack of knowledge of the English language. 'Sister Gulshan, how will you manage? You cannot speak English and you hardly know anyone over there.' At the heart of their prayers was their desire that Jesus would both equip me for the task he had given to me, and that he would go with me every step of the way.

My friends and I left at 4 o'clock on Sunday morning when it was still dark but cool. As we made our way along the Shahrah-e-Faisal road to the airport, jostling for space with tongas, rickshaws and bicycles, it seemed as if the whole of Karachi's population was on the move. The daily round and common task almost threatened to submerge them as they were all caught up in a hive of activity. They appeared to be moving to the beckoning of some unknown power co-ordinating their efforts.

I sat still, looking out of the car window at this energetic scene, feeling cool and detached, with my feet resting, as it were, on another plane. I too was being beckoned, but by no unknown power and for no ordinary task. Jesus, my Saviour, had given me a commission and my journey was being undertaken at his express command.

It is a beautiful and exhilarating feeling moving forwards towards one's destination as the dawn breaks. This special day and I seemed to greet each other as the darkness was gradually being overtaken by the clear light of day. I had been strengthened, and was encircled by the love of dear friends. How lovingly Patricia and her sister, Freda, had packed and repacked my case to make sure I had all I needed. They were both nurses in the Jinnah hospital, named after the founding father of Pakistan. Since that day, nearly a year before when I prayed for Freda and she was delivered from her illness, a strong bond of love has existed between us. Now this circle of love was interlocked into that greater circle of my Saviour's love.

Arriving at the airport, we all stepped out of the car and made our way towards the check-in counter. At the desk I handed in my one suitcase. I was travelling 'light', unlike those around me, who were laden with bags of various shapes and sizes. It was a noisy atmosphere; people were shouting and calling to each other. One voice rose above the rest: 'Shanti, did you pack those bracelets for Aunty?' Back came the slightly irritated voice: 'Yes. I have already told you six times!' Obviously, there were going to be some happy friends and relatives when these travellers arrived in Europe, I told myself.

For me, however, it was a trip into the unknown.

I had been in correspondence with one family, and I knew there was only one face I would recognize. Yet I was not completely alone. Deep within me there was the assurance that Jesus was with me and that he was in control of all that lay ahead of me. 'Lo, I am with you always', is the promise of his Word.

It was 6.30 a.m. when the call to board the aircraft was given and I stepped out of the airport building on to the tarmac and headed towards the plane. I was wearing my light blue shalwar kameeze and the ends of my dupatta fluttered gently in the cool breeze of this beautiful dawn. The Boeing 747 of Pakistan International Airlines was standing there like a giant mechanical bird waiting to whisk us across the skies and towards the West.

Clutching my one piece of hand luggage, with one hand, I reached for the rail as I put my foot on the first step leading up to the aircraft. At the top was one of the stewardesses dressed immaculately in the white and green of Pakistani Airlines. 'Welcome aboard,' she said warmly. I felt good. I had not been conspicuous, not been singled out for special attention, not needed anyone's assistance. Instead of drawing the usual compassionate look, I was greeted with a smile. That meant so much to me. At last I was just one of the crowd, doing naturally what everyone else was doing.

What a contrast this was to that first trip to England in the spring of 1966 when I was only fourteen. I was a cripple then, paralysed on my left side with only a wasted arm and leg – useless encumbrances. I had contracted typhoid when I was at the tender age of six months, and this had been followed by polio. I had never known what it felt like to get up and walk. The sight of other children walking, running, jump-

3

ing, the sound of their joyful voices delighted me, but also pained me. I used to say to myself, 'Such activities could never be part of my experience.' At least, so I thought then. I had never heard of Jesus Christ and did not know that one day he would be my Saviour and raise me up.

I made my way towards my seat and in no time at all I was settled and had fastened the seat beat. I glanced at my fellow passengers on either side and smiled; this time they were not the familiar faces of my two faithful maids, Salima and Sema, waiting eagerly to meet my every need. Neither was I travelling first class, with Father sprawled across the two seats in front of me. Not that I wouldn't have liked that. Father was the kindest, gentlest man I ever knew. The memory of his ever loving care always rouses tender feelings within me and I always felt secure in his presence. I can just see him now, striding ahead of me, well dressed as usual in his high-necked black overcoat, trimmed with gold buttons. He invariably walked ahead, clearing the way like some hunter wielding his cutlass through a thick tropical undergrowth.

It was now eleven years since I was healed but each time I go through a new experience, the initial joy of being in charge of myself, of being able to satisfy my basic human needs, floods my being afresh and my heart is lifted up in praise to him who has given me this new life. For nineteen long years I had had to suffer the indignity of being helped with the simplest of my desires. Now all that has changed.

My dear father, Aba-Jan, had not spared time or energy or expense to seek medical help for my stricken condition. I was the youngest of his five children and yet he had cared for me as if I were his only child. How faithfully he had kept his promise to my mother when, with her dying breath, she had given him a sacred charge: 'I beg you Shah-ji, do not marry again, for the sake of little Gulshan.' He never married again even though the Quran allows a man to have at least four wives. I believe that he would have cared for me just as well even without this promise.

That first trip in 1966 had been his last desperate attempt to find a cure for me. I remember how hopeful I was. In fact we all were hopeful as I was lifted on to the gangway in my wheelchair, that eloquent symbol of disability and dependence. Sadly, that hope had been dashed to pieces when, in our London hotel, Dr David had said, 'There is no medicine for this, only prayer.'

What strange words I thought then from the lips of someone who, in Father's eyes, was nothing but an infidel. But my father had not remained despondent for long. He had seized the doctor's last word with renewed zeal and enthusiasm to pursue it to its logical conclusion. I remember how he stroked my lifeless hand and said, 'There's only one way now. Let us knock on the heavenly door. We will go to Mecca as we intended. Allah will hear our prayers and we may yet return home with thanksgiving. The trip to Mecca which had been intended to be for thanksgiving for healing had then turned into a deeper search for the healing itself.

So it was that I, together with my father and my two maids, were caught up in the excitement of joining the annual pilgrimage to the holy shrine at Mecca. It still amuses me when I recall how Salima and Sema found it difficult to conceal their pleasure. 'How privileged we are to be going on a Hajj. All the girls in the village will envy us!' they cried out with delight. They

5

were fulfilling a dream which for so many others remains empty. Only the comparatively wealthy could fulfil this final pillar of Islam, the climax of their faith and all their aspirations.

But the heavenly door I was destined to knock on was not Mecca. I went to Mecca a cripple, and a broken-hearted cripple I returned to Pakistan, to see the undoubted look of disappointment on the faces of family and friends. In fact, now I was crippled in mind too. We had explored every avenue of help, human and divine, and faithfully performed all the prescribed rituals, only to be met with failure and even despair.

This bitter-sweet memory of my first trip was now tinged with a feeling of exhilaration. Those days are gone now. How like a bad dream they seem. This time I was going to England alone. God, my Creator, was now my Father and his presence was all I needed. I was not seeking to receive help, only hoping to give, to give a message from my Lord and Saviour Jesus Christ to his people. His words had burned themselves into my heart and now came afresh into my consciousness: 'What you have seen with your eyes, you must take to my people. My people are your people.'

As I leaned back in my seat, comfortable and relaxed, I said in my heart, 'Yes, Lord, I am going, bearing in my body the marks of my miraculous healing, to tell your people. Go ahead of me and prepare the way.' With that utterance a great feeling of peace, like a warm shower, flowed over me, enveloping my whole body. I took the blanket that had been given to me and drew it around me, wrapping it tightly as if to trap that wonderful feeling forever.

A smile rose to my lips. It was all so clear now, but oh, how dark it had been in the beginning. 'Lord, who are your people? Where are your people?' Had I not wrestled with these two questions day after day, night after night?

My aunt and uncle with their two children, distant relatives whom Father had welcomed into our home after the Partition with India in 1947, had stayed on to look after me after Father died. I remember distinctly my aunt's words to me when she saw me standing for the first time.

'It looks strange to see you stand. I have to get used to this,' she said as she enquired searchingly, 'How is it that your arm and leg are now normal, when for nineteen years they were withered and you a cripple?'

'Jesus has healed me and called me to be his witness,' I announced. Poor Aunty! Her bewildered look flashed into my mind. 'But there are no Christians here in Pakistan for you to witness to and you cannot go to America or England. Your witness should be to give alms to the poor. When these people come to you for food and money, that will be your witness.'

I had looked at her with amazement. She was not a particularly well educated woman, yet she had displayed great subtlety of mind. To her, no Muslim woman would dream of leaving the security of home, family and friends to go about preaching, and especially not abroad. She had decided what I should do – give alms (zakat) to the poor. Little did she know then that one day I would be dispossessed and would become one of the poor. My poverty would not lead, however, to my seeking alms; but, like the apostles Peter and John at the Temple, I would say to the poor, 'Silver and gold have I none . . .' and offer them the salvation wrought by Jesus Christ for us.

My father, a wealthy landowner and cotton farmer,

had become famous for his generosity. He did his best to fulfil this third Pillar of Islam. Giving was supposed to purify the giver. But it was not my 'purification' that my aunt was concerned about. I could fulfil Jesus' command, but only from the security of my home.

This had puzzled me. Jesus had expressly said to me, 'Tell my people.' How could his people be the poor Muslims who came to my door for alms, alms to which they felt entitled since the Quran enjoins the rich to share their wealth with the poor? I suspected that there was an unspoken fear that I would leave our ancestral faith and this had to be prevented at all costs. I had continued to give an annual zakat of 50,000 rupees since my father died and, within two or three weeks of my healing, I had increased this by 10,000. This had pleased my uncle who was now in control of my financial affairs.

'Listen Gulshan,' he said, 'whatever Jesus wants, you give it to him – land or money, but don't leave your country, or your religion, and above all, don't give yourself.' This was reiterated by my elder brother Safdar Shah, with an additional note of warning. 'Jesus has his people in England, America and Canada. These are Christian countries. You are not going there to tell them how Jesus has healed you and it would not be wise to broadcast that sort of thing over here.' So much for telling those who came for alms!

Such had been the admonitions and threats that I received from my family as I contemplated my Lord's commission. I became bewildered and confused. In desperation, I had cried out to Jesus, 'Show me your way, oh, show me your way.' Praise his name. He answered me in a most beautiful way.

While I was praying one day, I looked up and saw

a misty pillar, from floor to ceiling. Jesus was inside the mist. 'Come to me,' he said and gladly I rose and went. He put out His hand and I felt myself lifted off my feet as if I were in the air. I had shut my eyes and when I opened them I saw that I was standing on an open plain which stretched away in the distance, cool and green, and peopled with figures, some near and some in the distance. They all had crowns on their heads and were clothed in a brightness which hurt my eyes.

I heard the sounds of beautiful music and the people were singing, 'Holy' and 'Hallelujah', words wholly unfamiliar to me. I realized that they were looking at Jesus and saying, 'He is the slain lamb. He is alive.' Then Jesus said to me, 'These are my people. They speak the truth. They know how to pray, for they believe the Son of God.'

I knew then that his people were Christian people, and it was to them that I was to take his message. The darkness had at last been dispelled. I knew to whom I must go. This enlightenment brought so much relief that my heart sang with joy. The darkness did not depart without a struggle, however. I had still not been told where to go. That was to be discovered slowly and painfully.

After I was baptized, I wanted to give my testimony and Jesus' message to congregations of Christian people, but I was discouraged. The Pastor had said to me, 'You are not really ready for that. You have a witness in the home to fulfil. God will accept that.' Some time later he found a job for me as a house mother in the Sunrise School for the Blind.

On reflection, my experience there taught me how to rejoice in tribulation and suffering. Those young boys and girls did not spend their time moaning and

9

groaning under the burden of blindness. Instead, they discovered qualities in themselves which they never knew they had, and with these they explored new forms of happiness. The day would come when I too would learn that deeper joy and contentment.

My next job was perhaps stranger. I was employed as a reporter for a weekly magazine with offices in Old Anarkali Bazaar. In my desperation for a job (since I had to maintain myself), I had gladly accepted it. I learnt how to interview others and to keep accurate accounts of what was said to me. (This proved invaluable when I came to write my first book – *The Torn Veil*.)

What had seemed at first like distractions from my real task, in the end proved to be ways my Lord was using to prepare me for my future ministry. I knew that I had to submit and serve him in whatever situation I found myself, but I had to keep close to him if I were not to be diverted from the path he wanted me to tread. I had to be as strong as the first apostles who faced the same temptation when the gentile Christians murmured because their widows were being neglected in the daily administration. What did the apostles do? They summoned the people and said, 'It is not right that we should give up preaching the Word,' and added, 'but we will devote ourselves to prayer and to the ministry of the Word.'

It was not that being a kind of 'itinerant preacher' appealed to me. I had always been a shy and retiring sort of person. The long years of conditioning by my crippled state had reinforced my natural shyness. Public witness seemed alien to me; but I soon realized that when Jesus makes us 'new creatures', we become new indeed.

It was on 31st December 1975 that I received my

first invitation to give an address, in the church of the Foreman Christian College in Lahore. There had been no time to consider the implications of accepting, for I had to respond the very next day, 1st January 1976. That marked the beginning of my travels all over Pakistan addressing various groups and leading Bible classes. These travels took me to Muree, 8,000 feet above sea level in the foothills of the Himalayas. Later Rawalpindi became my base as I travelled to Karachi and other places.

Now, here I was in September 1982, some 30,000 feet above sea level and travelling at 500 miles per hour on the way to the very place my family were convinced I could never go. With the thought of this remarkable turn of events in my mind, plus all the good food we had been given on the plane, I must have fallen asleep. The next thing I heard was the Captain's voice saying that we should soon be landing at Heathrow Airport, London. He was precise and to the point, but it was enough to jolt me into reality. I was fully awake now. There was no turning back. My natural shyness surfaced momentarily, but the promise of Jesus – 'I will be with you always' – gave me the courage I needed.

Chapter 2

Arrival

After what seemed a long time, the door of the aircraft opened and we filed out. Once inside the airport building we followed the instructions leading to the immigration and passport control. A sense of excitement welled up inside me. At long last I would be able to fulfil the commission Jesus had given to me. I waited calmly in the queue. In the months following I was to learn how sacrosanct a queue is in England – no pushing or shoving, and certainly no breaking of the queue without incurring some very unpleasant looks.

When it was my turn, I presented my passport with my visa to the officer, who had an Asian interpreter with her. She looked at me, hardly smiling, and said quite firmly, 'You can stay in England for six months and after that you must leave the country.' She did not need to look so fierce and sound so commanding, I thought. 'I only want to stay for three months,' I announced boldly, so sure was I that after that time I should have accomplished my mission and would be on my way to Pakistan again. Whatever awaited me in England would not last long, I thought to myself reassuringly. This was not something premeditated. Why I said it I don't really know.

The immigration officer was flabbergasted. 'Why do you want to stay for three months when you have a visa for six months? Most people want to stay longer. You are the first person ever to have made such a request!' I realized I must have seemed odd to her, dressed in my shalwar kameeze and white coat and especially wearing dark glasses. 'Why have you come here?' the interpreter asked curiously. 'To serve God,' I replied undaunted. Back came the half-expected response. 'How can you serve God here? You do not speak English and you do not understand the customs and habits of the people.'

Hadn't I heard those very words once before? The words of the British Consul in Islamabad came forcibly back to my mind: 'You cannot speak English. How can you preach in England?' True, I did not speak English. Had not Father forbidden my teacher, Razia, to teach me English lest by learning the infidel language I should become contaminated with error and be drawn away from the faith? But neither he nor these people knew what Jesus could do. When he chooses people to do something in his name, he does not leave them helpless and unequipped for the job. He supplies all their needs.

I looked at the officer with a twinkle in my eye. Of course she could not see it because of my dark glasses! 'In Pakistan,' I said, 'I had the same problem. The Muslims did not understand me or my message. It will not be different here!' When the interpreter explained what I had said, she laughed and proceeded to stamp my passport for three months. Our little conversation must have relieved the monotony of her job. I could not help chuckling myself as I made my way towards the carousel to collect my luggage.

I picked up my suitcase when it appeared and went through the green channel. I did not need to be able to read the sign saying 'Nothing to declare'. Father had explained to me what it meant the first time I came here. I had so much to declare but nothing that would interest the authorities or fall within their banned list!

What a sea of faces greeted me as I emerged and glanced eagerly to see the one face I knew I would recognize. Then I saw my name written in bold letters on a board and held high above the heads of the crowd. Suddenly, there he was, a tall thin Englishman, Father Bernard himself.

He came forward to greet me. 'Sister Gulshan! At long last you are here! I cannot tell you how happy I am to see you again.'

'Father Bernard,' I said, 'this is a wonderful day for me. I am very pleased that our Lord Jesus Christ gave me permission to come. You and I know that this is all part of his plan.' 'Yes,' he said. 'I knew this from the moment I met you.'

That moment had been a year earlier. Father Bernard, an Anglican priest at the Community of the Resurrection, Mirfield, West Yorkshire, had been on a visit to Pakistan. He was staying with a friend of his who was a Roman Catholic missionary in the province of Sind, in Pakistan. When his friend became ill he took him to the St Raphael Hospital in Faisalabad. In England, Father Bernard had heard my testimony on tape but he had no idea where I lived. At the hospital he asked our Belgian doctor, Dr Elizabeth, 'Do you know a Sister Gulshan?' With sheer delight Dr Elizabeth had replied, 'Do I know her? She is my best friend. This hospital is more like her home. She lives near here.'

Father Bernard could not contain his excitement. 'Please, could you arrange for me to meet her as soon as possible?' 'Of course. I will arrange it straightaway.' Zenith, my adopted daughter, worked as a nurse in the hospital. Dr Elizabeth sent for her. 'Take my car and tell the driver to take you to your mother and bring her here,' she told Zenith. When Zenith walked through the door I was most surprised. 'Why are you here?' I asked urgently, thinking that this meant something was wrong. 'Are you not well? Only a few minutes ago you left for work.'

Zenith wasted no time on a lengthy explanation. 'Dr Elizabeth has sent me. She wants you at the hospital straightaway. It seems that there is a Father Bernard from England who wants to see you. He has heard a lot about you and cannot wait to see you.' Intrigued, I followed Zenith to the car and off we went. I had not at that time the slightest idea that that meeting would change the whole course of my life.

It was tea time when we arrived at the hospital and Dr Elizabeth had the tea table laid with sandwiches and cakes, a fitting welcome for our English guest. The tall thin gentleman came towards me beaming. 'Thank God, you have come. I feel sure that I have been guided to come here.' What was he talking about? I wondered. Why had he been guided to come here and meet me? I had no time to seek answers to these questions. There was a more pressing need at hand. Father Bernard asked, 'Will you pray for my friend? He has been having terrible stomach pains and nothing seems to relieve them.'

'Of course, I will pray for you friend,' I replied. I laid my hands on his friend's head and prayed for the wonderful healing power of Jesus to penetrate his body and make him whole. Later when Dr Elizabeth examined him she could find nothing wrong. 'Do you have any pain?' she asked him. 'No,' he replied, 'since Sister Gulshan laid her hands on me I have felt no

15

pain. Isn't it wonderful? I believe God has healed me!'

That brief encounter left Father Bernard in no doubt as to what his next step should be. We arranged to meet again the following morning. At ten o'clock I met him at the hospital. As soon as he saw me he said, 'I see Jesus' hand on you. I heard your remarkable testimony in England, but now I have seen with my own eyes what God is doing through you. Please, you must come to England and share your message with us.'

To England? I could not believe what I was hearing. This was the very place my family had said I could not visit. Was this really God's will for me?

I found myself answering, 'Thank you, Father Bernard. Thank you very much for your kind invitation. But first I must pray to Jesus. If he gives me permission I will come to England. I don't know how long it will take. But I do nothing without Jesus' permission. When I get that I will write to you. Please leave me your address.'

To my surprise he did not disregard my hesitation. 'Would you write to my friends in Huddersfield? They had expressly asked me to get in touch with you.' That was an invitation I could not refuse. I told my brothers and sisters in Christ that I would go to visit them when Jesus made his will clear to me. I encouraged them to continue to witness to Jesus Christ. This first message marked the beginning of a year-long correspondence with Uncle Hassan.

Up to that point I had been happy with the way my work had developed in Pakistan. I was witnessing to Jesus at conventions, addressing evangelistic meetings and leading Bible studies in churches. In everything I did, my one and only desire was to live in obedience to Jesus Christ.

> Trust and obey,
> There is no other way,
> To be happy in Jesus,
> But to trust and obey.

I learnt this hymn early in my Christian life. To leave Pakistan without first seeking Jesus' will was unthinkable. I prayed earnestly to Jesus for guidance on this matter and left it completely in his hands. In my heart I was prepared to accept whatever was his answer.

Several months passed, and still there was no light on the subject. There were times when it seemed that it was not God's will that I should go to England despite the urgent pleas from Uncle Hassan. But God works in his own mysterious way, according to his own timetable and not ours.

One year later I was praying at my usual time of 3.00 a.m., and I heard a voice saying, 'Go to England. I will be with you.' Any remaining doubt I had was dispelled. The next morning I wrote to Uncle Hassan, relieved that at last I could give him and the others the answer they had all been waiting for. 'My Master has given me permission to come to England. Please send me a sponsored letter and a return ticket.'

The green light had been switched on. All I needed now was a visa. I went to the office of the British Consul in Islamabad. In view of the clear command I had been given what followed seemed incredible. 'Why do you want to go to England?' the Consul asked me, not too kindly. 'To preach,' I replied calmly. He was taken by surprise. This was certainly not what he had expected. If I had said 'to study' or 'to join my family' he might have been more understanding and taken a different attitude. Instead he replied rather derisively, 'Missionaries come from England to Pakistan, not the other way round. In England there are many preachers. There is no need for you there. In any case, how can you preach over there? You speak no English.'

He refused to give me a visa. I committed this to Jesus. After all it was he who had told me to go. He would find a way. I remember leaving the Embassy with a peaceful mind. A greater power than the British Consul was in control of my life. This was in February 1982.

For the next three months I carried on with my preaching and teaching in various parts of Pakistan. Jesus was silent about England. In the summer I was preaching in Karachi. A second letter came from Huddersfield urging me to book my seat. I did! Visa or no visa I went to the Pakistan International Airlines office and booked my seat. I then wrote a letter to Uncle Hassan giving him the date and time of my arrival.

I was not one to flout the law, however, and go against the normal procedures, so I decided to make a second attempt to obtain a visa. I went to the Embassy in Karachi. When I got there I was both surprised and delighted to see the son of a Christian family, with whom I had stayed in 1981, working there. 'What are you doing here?' he asked with a big grin across his face. I explained to him my problem. 'Leave it with me,' he said reassuringly. He took my papers and translated the letter I had from Huddersfield for the Ambassador. He was a kind Christian man who was touched deeply by my testimony. He had no hesitation in granting me a visa for six months.

18

Within one week I had all that was necessary. I knew then, without a shadow of doubt, that divine providence had been at work preparing the way for me.

So, when Father Bernard and I greeted each other on that September day of 1982, it was in the confidence that our Father in heaven was at work in and through us. With this kind and generous-hearted priest were Anwar Kumar, Eric and Jacob, the three sons of Uncle Hassan. Uncle Hassan and I seemed to need no introduction except to look at each other – we recognized the author of our letters straight away. Dilip Kumar was the one who had actually sent me the sponsored letter to enable me to apply for a visa, so I thanked him warmly.

Father Bernard then addressed me: 'Sister Gulshan, I am sorry I cannot accompany you on your journey north this evening. I have an important engagement in London, but when I return to Huddersfield I will come to see you.'

The brothers and their father led me to their parked van. What a way to begin life here. I, a Muslim woman, was travelling alone with four men in one car. Clearly purdah did not apply here! Yet within a short time I was beginning to feel at ease with them. We spoke the same language and could talk freely and easily. The language barrier which had at first seemed the greatest obstacle to my mission in England was irrelevant at the moment. A short while ago we had been complete strangers and now we were like brothers and sister. Soon we were locked in a happy and animated conversation which lasted for the two and half or three hours' drive to Huddersfield. I saw the hand of Jesus in all this. He was working in our hearts and creating a warm friendship between us.

It was not long before the question which had been burning in their hearts came out almost spontaneously. 'Sister Gulshan, did it really happen as you said on the tape? Did Jesus really appear in your room and heal you?'

I smiled. These dear brothers in Christ were not doubting the truth of my testimony. It was just that they wanted to hear it from my own lips. They had waited a long time for this moment. 'Yes,' I answered gently, 'Jesus did appear to me in my room and He did touch me with His wonderful healing power. He made me whole. Praise his name!' 'Yes. Praise His name,' they all echoed almost simultaneously. They were content with that for the moment and relaxed as we sped up the motorway.

We stopped for tea at a motorway café. I felt somewhat conspicuous since we were the only Asians there. All the others were English. It was new for me, to see men and women sitting together and talking freely. In Pakistan, families normally sit secluded in little cubicles. When Anwar offered me tea, I felt shy and embarrassed to be on such easy terms with men. Eric, the sensitive one, was quick to spot my uneasiness and, putting his hand on my arm, said, 'Sister, we are your brothers. This is England.' Yes, indeed, I thought! This is England! It is no wonder that my family never wanted me to come over here. This initial reaction to life without the veil, without purdah, was soon whittled away however. I learnt to rejoice in the liberation which Jesus had given to me. He had truly torn the veil away. Why should I seek to hide myself again with it?

When we resumed our journey it was quite dark and I hardly noticed in which part of the country I was. Most of our conversation from then on centred on my companions' families, their wives and their children. By the time our journey ended I felt as if I knew them all intimately.

Chapter 3

At Huddersfield

We arrived in Huddersfield around 10.30 p.m. Eric parked his van outside his house, a three-bedroomed semi-detached house in a cul-de-sac. His wife Elizabeth, in good Indian tradition, greeted us at the door, since a guest must not arrive without being greeted at the door no matter what time of night it is. Eric's children, a four-year-old son and a five-year-old daughter, were already in bed. But Anwar Kumar's wife, his daughter and three sons were there to welcome me. Jacob's wife and Uncle Hassad's wife were on a visit to Pakistan.

Elizabeth had prepared chicken pilau and sweet rice for us, and soon I was sitting at the dining table having my first meal in England. We stayed up talking until 12.30. Inevitably, the conversation turned to the heart of what was on their minds – my encounters with Jesus Christ. To them I must have seemed like a first-century person stepping out of the pages of the New Testament. I had met and talked with Jesus.

They themselves had seen people being healed in services through the ministry of those specially gifted with the power of Jesus to bring healing to sick bodies. But in my case there had been no intermediary. Jesus himself had touched me. And that was before I even became a Christian! This was the extraordinary thing, the real miracle. I was not surprised when they said, 'Please, Sister Gulshan, forgive us for asking, but tell us again how you first met Jesus. Tell us from the beginning.'

So I began with the night after my father's funeral. 'From my earliest days, I have followed the custom of saying my prayers at three o'clock in the morning. That particular morning, instead of beginning my prayers I lay still for a while and waited to hear the sounds of the servants preparing for the day. Despondency seemed to fill me. The thought which came forcibly to my mind was the pointlessness of my continued existence. It seemed wrong that I, a cripple, should be alive, while Father, who was so good and kind, should be dead. Why hadn't I died instead? The world would not have missed me. What purpose was I serving?

' "Allah," I had said aloud, "I don't want to live like this for another thirty years. Please take me to father. With him I shall at least be happy." '

'You must have been desperately unhappy to pray like that,' someone said.

'Yes, I was, and I even began to have suicidal thoughts. God was silent and seemed so far away. He did not seem to want to help me so I thought I would have to rid myself of my suffering by other means. I considered hanging myself but this was impracticable since I only had use of one arm. I could not obtain poison or a knife either.'

'What a terrible thought! You would not have been able to join your father or your mother in Paradise if you had taken your own life.'

'That is true. Even if I failed to observe all the injunctions of Islam, I knew that as a member of a Sayed family, I had automatic right of entry to Paradise. Suicide would have deprived me of this right.' I recalled the scene at my father's deathbed. 'Weep-

23

ing, I had said to my father, "Father, if you go I will
follow you." Weak as he was Father said to me, "You
mustn't commit suicide. It is a sin. If you commit
suicide you will go to hell. Live a righteous life and
we will all be together with your mother." But my
despair knew no bounds. I was plunged into the deep-
est darkness and my tears flowed uncontrollably.
Death seemed the only way out. I cried out: "I want
to die. I don't want to live any more."

It was at that point that I had an awareness I had
never known before. Don't ask me how I knew but
deep down within me there was an unshakable assurance that I was being heard. This gave me a boldness
I would never have dreamt I had. I continued to talk
to whoever was listening.'

'Did you think this was Allah or Jesus?' asked Eric.

'I don't know what I thought, but I must have taken
this Being who was listening to me to be God, since
I found myself talking as if he had control over the
events of my life. Then I asked: "What terrible sin
have I committed that you have made me suffer like
this? Soon after I was born you took my mother away.
Then I became a cripple. Now you have taken my
father. Tell me, why are you punishing me like this?"'

Someone said to me at this point, 'That was a
strange way to talk to God. In all the Muslim prayers
you must have been taught from childhood, there was
nothing like this. What made you do it?'

'That I cannot explain. Following my outburst,
there was a deep silence. It was as if the whole uni-
verse had stopped for a while. Out of this stillness I
heard a low, gentle voice saying, "I won't let you die.
I will keep you alive."'

Here their curiosity took over. 'Could you hear the

voice with your ears or was it in your mind? In what language did it speak to you?'

'I heard it. It's hard to explain. It was like a breath of air passing over me but it was in my own language.'

'How did you feel? Did it make you happy?'

'I am afraid I had no time to consider my feelings. Besides, I wasn't too happy to be told that I would be kept alive. In my condition all I wanted was to die and go to Paradise, so I said, "What is the point of keeping me alive? I am a cripple. When my father was alive I could at least share everything with him. Now he is gone I have no hope and nothing to live for." Then I heard the voice again: "Who gave eyes to the blind? Who made the sick whole? Who healed the lepers and raised the dead? I am Jesus, son of Mary. Read about me in the Quran, in the Sura Maryam."

When I said this they could not contain their excitement. 'Oh, Sister Gulshan! What a wonderful experience that was! We wish Jesus would come and speak to us like that! But did you ever wonder whether you had just had a dream, that nothing really happened in reality?'

'Yes, I did for fleeting moments. The next day when we entered the forty days' mourning for my father, and I was caught up in the constant stream of relatives and friends coming to pay their respects to my father's memory, there were moments when my experience of the previous night did seem like a dream, but I was convinced that it wasn't.

'In the evening when all was quiet I asked my maid, Salima, to fetch my Quran and I tried to read the Sura Maryam. Despite the beautiful Arabic in which it is written I found it difficult to understand. Then the thought suddenly occurred to my mind. Why shouldn't I read it in my own language? After all, Jesus had addressed me in my own language. I decided to do just that. In the morning I called my maid and said to her: "Salima, would you go to the bookshop and buy me the best Urdu version of the Quran?" She seemed puzzled but said nothing, for my maids did not question my actions.'

'That was a brave thing to do,' one of the others said. 'As you know, Muslims believe that the Holy Quran can only be understood in Arabic. They don't think that it can be translated like any other book without losing some of its meaning.'

'Yes, I knew that but I was determined to understand what it said about this Jesus who had spoken to me.'

Uncle Hassan then asked: 'Had you never heard of Jesus before?'

'No. How could I have done? Confined as I had been to my bed and wheelchair and only meeting Muslims, I had never heard of Jesus. Since I could read the whole of the Quran from the age of seven I must have come across the name Jesus, but it didn't mean anything to me. At the first opportunity, I took my Urdu Quran, recited the Bismillah ("I begin this in the name of God the Compassionate, the Merciful") and found the Sura Maryam!'

One of them said: 'Let us see what it says.' Eric fetched his Quran.

The angels said to Mary:
Allah bids you rejoice in a Word from Him.
His name is the Messiah, Jesus the son of Mary.
He shall be noble in this world and in the next.
He shall be favoured by Allah.

He shall preach to men in his cradle and in the prime
of manhood
He shall lead a righteous life . . .

The wonder of it all filled our hearts anew. Here
was Jesus our Saviour, mentioned in the Quran itself,
Islam's holiest book and he is said to be favoured by
Allah!

This seemed a good point at which to bring our
conversation to an end. It was 12.30 at night and we
were all tired. We had had a long day. I went to bed
that night with peace in my heart. While I was resting
on the bed, the words of Jesus came clearly into my
mind: 'My people are your people.'

I heard Elizabeth's footsteps early next morning as
she came up the stairs and knocked on my door, a
cup of tea in her hand. 'Well, Sister, did you have a
good night?' she asked cheerfully as she placed the
cup on the bedside table. 'Yes, thank you,' I said, 'I
had a wonderful night's sleep. I feel so refreshed and
I am happy to be here.' 'Good. I am pleased. I will
see you later. I must go and get Miriam ready for
school.' With that she turned and left. I looked at the
cup of tea. How kind it was of her to bring it up but
somehow I must not let her know that I never have
a drink before I have washed and dressed and said
my morning prayers. Does a cup of tea involve so
many adjustments I wondered. What will I do when
the bigger issues present themselves?

I went downstairs just in time to see Miriam,
dressed in her school uniform and setting off for
school. For Pakistanis who have become Christians,
the question of their children wearing the school uniform instead of their traditional Pakistani dress does

not arise since for them the uniform symbolizes all the virtues which they prize such as discipline, respect for elders, and order in life.

Over breakfast, Elizabeth shared some of her experiences of living in England with me. 'When I first came here I could speak no English so I could not consider practising nursing here. In any case, Eric did not want me to go out to work. You know how it is with our men; they like their wives to remain at home and look after the home and the children. I did not mind as I liked being at home and seeing only members of the family. I felt secure.'

'Miriam looked nice in her uniform,' I said, reflecting that if she were in Pakistan she might not have been sent to school. 'Oh yes, she loves her school. We are very fortunate. But for me the most important thing is that when the children are ill I don't have to worry where I shall get the money from to take them to the doctor's. Eric pays National Insurance contributions and these cover the cost of visits and medicines. Life is getting better for us.'

'But it was not always as easy,' added Anwar's wife, who had come over to visit. 'We hardly saw our husbands at first. They had to work very hard to establish themselves, sometimes doing two jobs, one at night and one in the day. The only times we saw them and could be together was at the weekend. It was a high price to pay but at least we did not have the constant worry of where the next meal was coming from. What I like most of all, though, is that this is still a Christian country and we can practise our Christianity freely without fear of persecution and harassment. We do sometimes get into conflict situations with our fellow Pakistanis who are still fiercely Muslim, but we know that they cannot harm us.'

Yes, I thought that must be a blessing indeed, considering all I had to suffer even from my own family.

Eric and his brothers did not get up early because they worked at night. After lunch, they all came together again and we sat in Eric's front room. From the look on their faces I could tell that they were eager for me to continue from where I had left off on the previous evening. Eric, as usual, was the first to ask: 'For how long did you read the passages in the Quran about Jesus? Did anyone know you were doing this?'

'For three years I read and reread the passages concerning Jesus. I found that the best time for me was after my aunt's children had gone to bed and the house was quiet after the last prayer call. What puzzled me was the fact that someone so great as Jesus should have had so little written about him. I asked Aunty one day: "Do you know anything about Jesus?" The look on her face told me she was not very pleased that I was interested in Jesus but she answered all the same. "He's the only prophet in the Quran who gives eyes to the blind, raises the dead, and who is coming again. But I don't know in which Sura this can be found."'

My audience gave out sounds of great surprise. 'How did she come to know this about Jesus?' Now I come to reflect upon it, it was strange that she should know so specifically this particular piece of information about Jesus.

'Did nothing else happen to you in those three years while you were reading about Jesus? After all it was a long time and the verses are short.'

'No, nothing happened, but my meditation upon those verses had implanted hope within me which refused to die. I knew in my heart that if anyone

29

could heal me, he could. I began to believe that what was written about Jesus was true and that he did work miracles; but the waiting was becoming intolerable.'

'What happened after three years?'

'I started to pray to Jesus directly. "O Jesus, son of Mary, it says in the Holy Quran that you have raised the dead and healed the lepers. Please heal me too." '

'Did you pray any other prayers? Did you abandon your Muslim prayers?'

'No, not at first. I continued to use the prayer beads I had brought home from our pilgrimage to Mecca. I used to repeat the Bismillah after each prayer but then I began to add after each prayer, "O Jesus, son of Mary, heal me." This prayer took such a hold on me that before I knew it I was praying it between prayer times and even on each bead.'

'Your crippled condition must have grieved you considerably for you to plead for healing in the way you did. Yet you were not poor or homeless,' commented one of the others.

'But it was not only my physical condition which bothered me. My mind was becoming crippled too. I had lost all sense of the meaning and purpose of life. What use was a helpless cripple to the world? I was becoming overwhelmed by my helplessness and also becoming spiritually dead. I needed to be rescued from this pitiful condition.'

The others were getting a bit impatient. They wanted me to tell them what happened next. So I explained: 'One morning I was awakened at three o'clock as usual and I was sitting up in bed reading. Deep within me, however, was the constant prayer for Jesus to heal me. Then suddenly I deliberately stopped myself. A series of questions rose up within me. Why hadn't I been healed? I had been praying for three years. I had read the Suras in the Quran which Jesus himself had instructed me to read. Why had he not healed me? Why did he lead me to hope that he would? I addressed him boldly: "Jesus, I know that you are alive. You have spoken to me. It says in the Holy Quran that you have healed people. You can heal me and yet I am still a cripple? Why?" But only silence greeted my outburst. I cried out again in despair: "If you are able to, heal me, otherwise tell me why not. I cannot go on like this."

'Suddenly my whole room was flooded with light. At first I thought it must be the light from my reading lamp but its light was dim. Then it occurred to me that it might be the outside light switched on by the gardener to protect the ripe mangoes from thieves or to water the garden in the cool of night. But the shutters were closed and the curtains drawn. I became afraid and covered myself with my shawl. Something impelled me to look, however. The light was growing brighter and brighter until it surpassed the light of day.

'Slowly, I became aware of figures in long robes standing in the midst of the light, a few feet away from my bed. There were twelve figures in a row and the figure in the middle, the thirteenth, was larger and brighter than the others. By now I was trembling with fear and cried out: "Oh God! Who are these people? How have they come in here when all the windows and doors are shut?"

'Suddenly, a voice said: "Get up. This is the path you have been seeking. I am Jesus, son of Mary, to whom you have been praying and now I am standing in front of you. Get up and come to me."

I began to weep. "Oh Jesus, I am crippled and I

31

can't get up," but he merely repeated; "Stand up and come to me. I am Jesus."

'I hesitated. He said the same words a second time. When I still doubted, he said a third time the same words. Slowly I began to feel new strength flowing into my wasted limbs. I put my foot on the floor and stood up. Then I ran and fell at his feet. I was bathed in the purest light which seemed to burn as if the sun and moon were both shining together. This light seemed to penetrate into my heart and many things became clear to me at that moment.

'Jesus put his hand on the top of my head and I saw a hole in his hand from which a ray of light shone down upon my garments so that my green dress looked white. He said: "I am Jesus. I am Immanuel. I am the Way, the Truth, and the Life. I am alive and I am coming soon. From today you are my witness. What you have seen now with your eyes and what you have heard with your ears you must take to my people. My people are your people. From now on you must keep this robe and your body spotless. Wherever you go I will be with you and from today you must pray like this:

Our Father, which art in heaven,
Hallowed be thy name.
Thy kingdom come.
Thy will be done, on earth as it is in heaven.
Give us this day our daily bread.
Forgive us our trespasses, as we forgive those who
    trespass against us.
Lead us not into temptation, but deliver us from evil.
For thine is the kingdom, the power and the glory,
Forever and ever,
Amen."

Then I looked at my arm and leg. There was flesh on them now. Although my arm now had strength and was no longer withered, it was not perfect. So I asked Jesus: "Why don't you make it whole?" Jesus replied lovingly: "I want you to be my witness."

'With that, the light began to fade and the figures were vanishing. I longed to prolong the vision but it was no use. The light went and I found myself alone in the room, wearing a white garment. My eyelids were heavy from the dazzling light, so that even the dim light from my bedside lamp hurt my eyes. I groped towards a chest of drawers which stood against the wall. In a drawer I found a pair of sunglasses which I used to wear in the garden. I put them on and then found that I could open my eyes without discomfort. I looked at my clock. It was four o'clock in the morning.'

Everyone fell silent, each wrapped in his or her own thoughts, thinking about the Jesus to whom they too had committed their lives. He was real. He was alive. He knew each one intimately. I could see how overwhelmed they were with the wonder of it all. When Elizabeth offered to make a cup of tea, they all sighed with relief as if my story had been too much to take in in one go. There were big smiles on everyone's face.

Chapter 4

Conversation with Muslims

Having heard my testimony from my own lips, Uncle Hassad and his sons were now more than ever anxious that I should meet a group of fellow Pakistanis who worked as bus drivers. These Pakistanis were staunch Muslims with whom my friends were in constant discussions, sometimes very heated ones, about Jesus and why they had become Christians. The Hassans had played the tape recording of my testimony to them but these faithful followers of Muhammad said they would only believe if they saw me in person. It was this which had at first prompted Uncle Hassan to invite me over.

A meeting was arranged for Friday afternoon. It was to be in Eric's front room. The chairs were set out so that I would be facing my visitors. Eric expected six men. Muslim women would not normally join such a gathering even though I was going to be there. This was not anything personal, since they do not go to the Mosque on Fridays but stay at home and say their prayers. Even in social gatherings they tend to segregate. I was not surprised that none of the men brought their wives.

Eric sat on one side of me and Uncle Hassad on the other. A Christian friend of Eric's called Yacub was also there. This sign of physical and moral support was meant to give added weight to what I had to say. When the men entered and sat down they gave me such a searching look that I felt totally exposed. For

34

one fleeting moment I wished I still wore the veil as they studied me from head to toe. No part of me seemed to escape their penetrating gaze. They were probably making sure, I thought, that I was real and not a figment of anyone's imagination.

Eric left them in no doubt. 'This is Sister Gulshan, whose testimony you heard on the tape.' They looked slightly uncomfortable. It was as if they still could not believe that the offhand challenge they had casually thrown out had really been taken up. Confronted with the reality, they had to say something.

'Is it really your voice on the tape?' one of them asked.

'Of course it is,' I replied calmly. 'Listen for yourselves.'

'Are you really who you say you are? Is it true that you are from a Sayed family?'

I was a little taken aback. It was not my testimony they were interested in but my credentials. I had to establish who I was, who my family were. But I had no hesitation in answering. 'I was born Gulshan Fatima, the youngest daughter of a Sayed family. I was named after Fatima, daughter of the Prophet Muhammad. We were proud that we could trace our ancestral line through his son-in-law, Ali. My father was the head of the family. He was also a religious leader, a Pir, and even the Mullahs consulted him on important religious questions.'

'Where did you live?' they wanted to know.

'We lived in Jhang city in the Punjab. Jhang as you know, is about 250 miles from Lahore. My father was a landlord with a large estate in the country. Our huge bungalow surrounded by beautiful gardens was on the edge of the city.'

'But how do we know that you are not making all this up? What proof have you got that all this is true?'

The implication that I was a liar hurt me very much but too much was at stake for me to worry about my hurt feelings so I answered. 'Why would I want to make all this up? If you don't believe me, if you won't accept what I say about myself, you could write to my two brothers and sister. I will give you their addresses.'

They didn't take up this offer, but asked instead, 'If your family are alive and well, why did you leave them? Did they not love you?'

'My family loved me deeply. There was nothing my father would not have done to help me, to ease the burden of my crippled state. I had two maids constantly by my side to see to my every need. We had several servants who did all the household chores. Even when Father could have remarried, he didn't lest a stepmother should have ill-treated me.'

Their look softened a little. They all must have known, even if not at first hand, of the problems of having stepmothers. 'If your family loved you as much as you say, why did you leave them?' they asked.

They couldn't have listened carefully to my tape, I thought. 'I had to obey Jesus Christ. He called me to be his witness. I had to take his message to his people.'

'But you could have witnessed by staying with your family. You said that they were wealthy. You could easily have found another way, surely?'

'You don't understand. My family threatened to kill me if I continued to say that Jesus Christ healed me. How could I continue to live with them?'

'Perhaps you were not healed. Were you really a cripple for nineteen years?'

How ironic, I mused. My own family did not question my illness or the reality of my cure. All they wanted was for me to say that Muhammad healed me and not Jesus Christ. These men wanted me to say that I was never really ill!

'Why should I lie about my crippled condition?' I asked in disbelief. 'Do you really think that I would lie about something like that? It is nothing to be proud of. Anyway, there are people in Jhang who would confirm my crippled condition.'

They got somewhat irritated. 'All right, all right, so you were healed of a crippled condition. Why do you have to make so much fuss about it? Other people get healed, but they don't go around making up all sorts of stories about their healing.'

This distressed me. I could see the hurt look on the faces of my friends. I think they would have ended the discussion right then if I hadn't continued to answer these men calmly.

'You don't understand, do you? It is not just my healing that I talk about. It is the message of salvation that Jesus gave me for his people that I am delivering.'

'What message? Jesus' message is not important to us. Our prophet Muhammad (may peace and blessings of Allah be upon him) is greater than Jesus. He is the last Prophet of Allah and we obey his message. We don't need any other.'

'But don't you pray night and day, "Guide us in the straight path, The path of those whom you favour?" Well I am telling you, if you want this prayer to be answered, you must believe in Jesus Christ. Jesus is the Way, the Truth, and the Life. He is the straight path, the path to God our Father.'

'Do you dare to call Allah "Father"? This is blasphemous. Now we know for sure that you could not

37

have been a Muslim. You must have been brought up as a Christian. No good Muslim would dare to do such a thing. You are mad. Only men can be fathers. Allah is not a man.'

'Jesus told me to call God "Father". In the Bible it says: "But as many as received him (i.e. Jesus) to them, God gave the right to become the children of God" [John 1: 12]. The beautiful prayer Jesus himself taught me begins: "Our Father . . ." Jesus called God "Father" and he has given us the same privilege. It is only through the Spirit of the Son of God that anyone can call God "Father". You cannot call him "Father" because you have not the Spirit within you.'

They were speechless for a moment. Then one of them said: 'Our Quran does not teach us to call Allah our father. In the Quran there are ninety-nine beautiful names for God: "Al-Raham" (The Merciful), "Rahim" (The Compassionate) "Al Malik" (The Sovereign) and many many others. Were these not good enough for you? If you want to believe the Bible and follow its teachings, then it is up to you. You were probably not a good Muslim anyway.'

They seemed to excel in saying the most hurtful things.

'How could you say that? I was as good a Muslim as any of you. My father drilled into me the Catechism, just as your father probably did. I knew it off by heart. Even now I can hear my father asking:

"Where is Allah?"

"Allah is everywhere."

"Does Allah know all the actions you do on earth?"

"Yes. Allah knows all the actions I do on earth, both good and bad. He even knows my secret thoughts . . ."

'You don't need to go on. We can see that you

learnt all this. You obviously did not learn the most important thing. Does not the Shahada say: "There is no God but God (Allah) and Muhammad is his Prophet (Peace be upon him)?" '

I looked at these faithful followers of Muhammad with love in my heart. I knew that, like my father, they loved their religion and nothing gave them greater pleasure than to do their ablutions and say their prayers. I was not a mere observer. I could feel what they were feeling.

'For nineteen long years I believed the Shahada and I still believe that there is only one God but I also believe that Jesus is the Son of God, and not just a prophet as the Quran says.'

'Are you saying that Jesus Christ is greater than our Prophet?'

'I am saying that Jesus Christ is no mere prophet. He is the Son of God who is the Way, the Truth and the Life. He is the way to God the Father.'

'If you were such a good Muslim how is it that you thought of committing suicide because you were not healed? That showed a rebellious spirit. You should have submitted to Allah's will. If Allah wanted you to remain a cripple, then you should not have rebelled against his will. After all, the very essence of Islam is submission.'

'It was not that I was rebelling. I just could not see the point of my continuing existence. What use was I to myself or to anyone else?' I asked, feeling very sad that, instead of rejoicing, people regretted my healing. This would not be the first time that I would encounter such an attitude.

'Allah would have decided that!' they echoed one after another.

'Maybe. But all I know is that Jesus decided. He

reached down to a despairing Muslim girl and recreated my crippled body and turned it into a body of wholeness and strength. The message he has given me for his people I must give, whatever the cost,' I said resolutely.

'But your own flesh and blood rejected you. Your brothers and sister still do not believe in Jesus do they? And do you expect us to believe?' they asked in amazement.

Suddenly they changed the subject. 'What do you think about the veil? Does not the Quran say: "Prophet, enjoin your wives, your daughters, and the wives of true believers to draw their veils close round them. That is more proper so that they may be recognized and not molested." How is it that you who claim to be a member of a Sayed family, have discarded the veil?' they asked almost triumphantly.

'It was to protect women from men's lustful eyes that the veil was introduced. You know that in many Muslim countries today it is no longer worn. If men could control their thoughts women wouldn't have had to resort to the yashmak [the veil worn by Muslim women in public] or any of the other devices to protect themselves.'

This brought forth some angry looks. Not only was I seeming to attack their religion but I was questioning their customs and traditions as well. No wonder they retorted: 'We don't need you to tell us what to believe or what traditions to uphold.'

'You are quite right. You don't need me, but you do need Jesus Christ to forgive you your sins. He died on the cross for your sins,' I said.

Back came their confident answer: 'We don't need anyone to die on a cross for us. Allah has promised to forgive us our sins, and to take us to Paradise when we die. We know where we are going. Do you know where you are going?' they asked rather arrogantly.

'I am as sure as anyone can be that when I die I shall go to heaven to be with Jesus. In 1971 on the 8th January, while I was still in Pakistan, I had a vision of heaven. In it I saw a beautiful gate and beyond it a host of people all dressed in white, praising God. I saw myself among them.'

'We are not interested in visions' they said derisively.

'But Muhammad had visions. Do you not believe in them?' I asked.

This made them angrier. 'You don't mean to tell us that you are putting your vision on the same level as our Prophet's, do you? Now we have heard everything. What is the good of talking to you?'

Eric couldn't stand it anymore. At this point he got up and went to fetch the tea from the kitchen where Elizabeth had been busy preparing it. The men saw a chance to tempt me. 'Look, why don't you give up all this talk about Jesus and return to Islam? If it is love you need or money you want, we will give you everything,' they said, this time smiling hopefully.

They underestimated me. 'Even if you gave me the whole world I would not give up following Jesus Christ and obeying him. Jesus Christ died for my sins and has reconciled me to God our Father and he has promised me eternal life. What more could I possibly want? You will die one day but Jesus will always be with me. He supplies all I need. I love Jesus.'

Now they too had had enough. 'This is beyond our thinking. But if this is how you feel, then you can die in your Christianity!' With that, they all stood up and marched out.

When Eric returned with the fully laden tray, he

was astonished. The room was empty of visitors. They had all gone. His eyes widened and his mouth opened wider and wider. He was speechless and nearly dropped the tray. When he had regained his composure, he put the tray on the table and sat down. 'What happened?'

'They couldn't take anymore.'

'But I thought . . .'

'I know what you thought. You believed that, confronted with me in the flesh, they could not possibly fail to believe. You were probably hoping for too much. Unbelief is a mystery. Some won't believe because they want evidence that would convince them and others reject the evidence they have.'

Uncle Hassan, with more experience and the wisdom of age, added: 'I am afraid it is not as simple as that. You see, for these Muslims, it is much more than their religion which is at the heart of their resistance to Christianity. Their fierce and almost fanatical adherence to Islam with its straightforward beliefs, traditions and customs, gives them a sense of dignity and an identity which is crucial for their survival, as they see it, in a foreign country. Without this they feel that they would be reduced to being mere second class citizens, forever confined to doing all the menial jobs that nobody else wants to do.

'They don't feel like an isolated immigrant group any longer. They belong to a world wide community of brothers. Have you not seen the beautiful mosques being put up everywhere? Some people believe that most of the money for these comes from abroad. Muslims now know that they can call on their brothers in the richer countries to help and support them. So, you see, to give up Islam is to give up a great deal more than just a religion.'

Yes, I thought, the cost of discipleship is high indeed. I opened my Bible and read Mark 8: 34–38:

And Jesus called to him the multitude with his disciples and said to them, 'If any man would come after me, let him deny himself and take up his cross and follow me. For whoever would save his life will lose it; and whoever loses his life for my sake and the gospel's will save it. For what does it profit a man to gain the whole world and forfeit his life? For what can a man give in return for his life? For whoever is ashamed of me and of my words in this adulterous and sinful generation, of him will the Son of Man also be ashamed when he comes in the glory of his Father with the holy angels.'

We enjoyed the tea Elizabeth had so lovingly prepared but in a rather quiet and subdued manner. We had a lot to think about.

Chapter 5

Mission Begins

True to his word, on the following day at 4.00 p.m. Father Bernard arrived. He was delighted to see how warmly I had been received. He had supper with us. To my surprise I heard him saying, 'This is good; very tasty.' He was certainly enjoying Asian food. I could see from the way he tucked in that he was not just being polite. After supper, Anwar and Eric had to leave for work. Father Bernard stayed on.

'Sister Gulshan, we must plan a programme for you,' he announced. He did not want me to waste any time but to get on as soon as possible with fulfilling the task I had been given to do, and in which he was going to play his part.

'What I will do is this. I will write to churches all over Britain and encourage them to invite you. I am sure that there are Christians all over the country who will rejoice to meet you and hear your testimony.'

That night I committed all this to the Lord. During the day when I was on my own I would spend my time reading my Bible and praying. 'Lord,' I would say, 'you brought me here to England. For eleven years you prepared me for this. Give me wisdom that I may serve you in ways that are pleasing to you, and strength and courage to do what I have to do well. I want only your name to be glorified.'

Praise his name! He did show me. Doors began to open all over the country. Travelling by coach and train was to become as familiar to me as the tonga and the rickshaw in Pakistan. The sight of me in my shalwar kameeze, dupatta, white coat and dark glasses must have evoked curious glances in my direction. I was certainly not inconspicuous, even though I did not set out to be noticed.

For the next three days I was able to relax and soak in the atmosphere of the place. I had not expected to see such a variety of nationalities – Asians, Jamaicans, and even some Chinese people. Every variety of dress greeted me. What a colourful sight it was. My first meetings had been arranged for the weekend, on Friday, Saturday and Sunday evenings. As we drove around Huddersfield I saw posters advertising these meetings and my name in bold letters staring at me from several shop windows. Are they really about me, I wondered. The tempter was not far away.

'Of course they are about you. You are special and you are going to be famous one day.'

'But I don't want to be famous,' I argued. 'I want Jesus Christ to be glorified in my life. I am only here because He has brought me. It is His name which should be displayed prominently. I am nothing.'

The tempter reminded me, 'Do you not recall the story your family told you about the time when your parents took you, soon after you were born, to the najumi? How he read your little palm and predicted that you were going to be famous one day? Well, that day has arrived.'

Deep within me another voice seemed to be saying to me reassuringly: 'Listen, Gulshan, point people to Jesus Christ. That is what you have to do. He needs you to do the pointing. You are his instrument, however unworthy you feel.'

'Yes, Lord,' I responded, 'that is just what I want to be, your instrument. And what an instrument – a withered body restored to life. You can have me, all of me, to play your tune upon. Your Gospel will resound from every fibre of my being.' Then the tempter left me.

I looked forward to addressing my first audiences in the hall of the Elim Pentecostal Church. This seemed to be the most natural place to start. Of all Christian groups, the Pentecostals are the ones who still believe passionately that Jesus works miracles today. Miracles for them did not cease with the Apostolic age. This belief seems to penetrate their souls to such an extent that their worship is characterized by joyful singing, hand clapping, extempore prayer, interspersed with ejaculations of 'Praise the Lord' and 'Hallelujah'. I had encountered this type of service in Pakistan so it was not new to me.

The night for my first public address in England arrived. There were at least one hundred people there, almost all English. I recalled that, never in all the years in Pakistan, had it occurred to me that one day I would be speaking to an English audience. For me this amounted to a miracle.

I addressed them through an interpreter. It was interesting to listen to him as he tried to keep up with my racy style of speaking and it also gave me breathing spaces! There seemed to be some power pushing me on and my testimony held the audience spellbound. It confirmed so much of what they believed: that Jesus hears and answers prayers today; that there is no barrier he cannot penetrate, even the barrier of a strong Islamic faith. No veil, whether of religion or culture or ignorance, which hides the truth concerning himself is too strong for him to tear away. They became excited by Jesus' message that **He is alive and He is coming soon**. Many felt impelled to commit themselves to him anew with zeal and enthusiasm.

My next meetings were held in the Church of God, another branch of the Pentecostal denomination. Most of its members come from the black community. In fact the Church of God is the largest and most influential black Pentecostal body in the world. The congregation here were mainly Jamaicans. They were even livelier than the Elim Pentecostals!

At the end of one of these services, during question time, someone got up and asked me: 'Sister Gulshan, why did you address Jesus as Son of Mary?'

I had never considered how unusual this must have sounded to people who had become accustomed to addressing Jesus as Son of God, Saviour, and Lord. My reference to Jesus as Son of Mary must have sounded like a demotion of him and yet nothing could have been further from the truth. Ironically this fits in well with the Quran's view of Jesus. I tried to answer my questioner as simply as I could.

I related how I first learnt the title and added: 'Remember, that at this time I knew nothing about Jesus. The only religious book I had was the Quran, and here Jesus is called the son of Mary. It is true that the Quran acknowledges that Jesus' birth was special in that there was no man involved, but it sees no special significance in this, since unusual events are nearly always said to accompany God's special messengers. On this view Jesus is on the same level as Adam, Abraham, Moses or even Muhammad. So you see, it was only when Jesus appeared to me in my room that I began to understand who he really was.

'The light which shone into my room shone in my heart and mind also and I saw clearly that Jesus was not a mere man but the Son of God, the Lamb who was slain for my sins and the sins of the whole world. I had been taught that we needed to sacrifice an animal in order to gain forgiveness of sins. That is why at Bacha Id each member of the family offers a goat. As the blood of the animal flows away, so our sins are taken away. This we had to do year after year. Now I saw Jesus as the one who by his own death, once for all on the cross, had washed away my sins.

'This only became clearer to me as I read the Bible. The Quran teaches that Jesus was not truly crucified. He escaped. God, the Quran says, saved Jesus from the hands of the Jews who wanted to put him to death. Another victim was substituted in his place. Jesus was the son of Mary, and Mary was not Haroon's sister, as the Quran says, but a descendant of David.'

I was very pleased with this opportunity to explain what I had learnt about Jesus Christ, and not to have to concentrate wholly on my healing experience. This greatly encouraged me.

On Wednesday 6th October I was invited to meet with a group of Pakistani Christians in Nelson in Lancashire. This was my first trip outside Huddersfield. Strange new names were being added to my vocabulary and written in my diary every week.

These believers shared with me some of their problems in continuing to believe in the basic truth of Christianity. 'Our fellow Pakistanis who have remained Muslims continually accuse us of believing in three gods. We find it very hard to explain to them that we don't. How does one explain the Trinity when we find it difficult to understand ourselves? They say that like the Arabs before Muhammad we are worshipping three gods rather than one. They remind us that the Arabs worshipped Al IIah, Al Lat, and Al

Uzza. It seems to make no sense to them that the Trinity is not three gods but One God in Three Persons?

Such theological questions were not the only problems facing Pakistani Christians – as I discovered in the following months. The practical ones were even more difficult. All I could do to help was to share my experiences of Jesus Christ with them and encourage them to hold on, because as Jesus had told me to say: **He is alive and He is coming soon**.

My ministry was not confined, however, to addressing Pentecostals and Pakistani Christians. On my return from Lancashire, I addressed audiences in three Anglican churches. Elizabeth and Eric accompanied me, and Eric acted as my interpreter. Here the congregations were more subdued but listened politely and many expressed warm feelings of appreciation at the end of the services.

Later in the month, on 17th October, I visited one of the most interesting cities I was ever privileged to see – Oxford. It was a place I knew by name, for its reputation as a place of academic excellence had penetrated even the most remote villages of Pakistan. Anyone who was clever or ambitious enough dreamed of going to Oxford to study.

My brother Alim Shah had come from Pakistan to study Law here, and had painted a picture of a beautiful city with its magnificent architecture. I had only to look at its fine buildings as we drove along to see what he meant. I remember him adding, 'Of course, it is also a city full of infidels if its great number of church spires is anything to go by!' I have learnt since that those very spires have been a rich source of inspiration evoking poetic descriptions, some of them

even immortalized, like the one which describes the
city as 'the city of dreaming spires'.

These spires were anything but dreaming when I
first saw them. The sight of them thrilled me, and I
lifted up my heart to heaven in thanksgiving for my
creation – which is what they were constructed to do.
I did not know it then but this was a place which was
destined in the providence of God to have a significant
place in my life. As my knowledge of the city has
increased over the years, I have discovered how eloquent has been its witness to the Christian faith. Was
it not here that John Wycliffe first translated the Latin
Bible into the English language so that ordinary
people could read it? How thrilling it must have been
for them! I remember how from the age of seven I
had read the Quran in its beautiful Arabic poetry and
had loved it. But when I wanted to understand its
meaning I had secretly purchased a copy in my own
native tongue in order to know its contents.

As I was taken to the house of my guest, we had a
tricky time avoiding the hordes of cyclists on the
road. Any moment I thought we would hit one. They
seemed to be all over the place, weaving their way
about, with their black gowns trailing in the wind
behind them. I was amazed. I thought that people
only rode bicycles in such numbers in Pakistan!

My host for the weekend was the Pastor of the
Asian church. This had been arranged by Father
Bernard. I was delighted to meet the Pastor,
especially as he too was the only member of his
Muslim family to become a Christian. Most Pakistani
and Indian Christians are from families who were
converted to Christianity by European missionaries
during the last century. I felt I had much in common

with the Pastor whose family greeted me and welcomed me warmly into their home.

St Luke's Church in Canning Street had been hired
for the meetings which had been scheduled for me.
Normally the Asians meet for worship in a Baptist
Church in Witham Street and their main service is
held at 3.00 p.m. Many of these Christians had already
heard my testimony on tape; but, as elsewhere, they
were eager to hear it from me personally.

On the first night, as the Indian women walked
elegantly into the church wearing their colourful and
beautiful saris, I felt as if I had been transported back
to India. In Pakistan I saw only the Pakistani dress.
A lot of them, I later learnt, had come from the
Punjab, many from the same area, even the same
villages. They were a very close knit community.

It was a very moving experience for me as I stood
up to address them, recalling in my mind the words
of Jesus, 'My people are your people.' From every
nation, from every tribe he had called them. A vision
of heaven flashed before my eyes. How thrilling it
would be when, clad in our white gowns, our distinc-
tions obliterated, we shall stand before the heavenly
throne and sing to the Lamb who was slain for us.
We shall not need interpreters then, as for the first
time I did not need one now.

The service was conducted in Punjabi and I spoke
in Urdu, both languages easily understood by my
audience. The sounds of the Indian instruments – the
dolki, the cabaza, the maracas, the tambourine, the
tabla and the accordion resounded through the building, lifting our hearts in praise and adoration of our
Saviour.

The choirmaster, a young and enthusiastic Christian man, came up to me afterwards and said: 'Sister

Gulshan, I work at Radio Oxford on the Woodstock Road. I can arrange for you to be interviewed for a special programme which goes on the air every Christmas.'

I could hardly believe my ears. I, Gulshan Esther, witnessing to Jesus over the Radio in England! What would my family have said if they heard this? I agreed enthusiastically. What better time, I thought, could there be to tell of the wonderful healing power of Jesus which had wrought such a glorious miracle in my body? But even more glorious would be the opportunity to penetrate the sentimentality which surrounds Christmas with the wonderful proclamation: **I am the Way, the Truth, and the Life**. This alone would enrich the light of all those lights which shine so beautifully at Christmas and restore the true meaning and significance of this special Christian festival.

The director of the programme agreed and it was arranged that the choirmaster would ask the questions. The night before it I prayed to Jesus: 'Lord, I am nothing. Use me to glorify your name.' The Pastor took me in his car to the station. I was a little nervous. I had never been in a recording studio before in my life. I was introduced to the English director who showed us into the recording room. The choirmaster was there. He explained the procedure to me.

'I will ask a question. When you answer you speak into this microphone. I will lift my finger when I want you to stop speaking. This is necessary for you to remember because you will be wearing these headphones. Try them on. We shall have a practice session first.'

He put such questions to me as: Where was I born? Who were my family? What was wrong with me?

How did I come to be healed? Who did I think had healed me? My answers had to be short and precise. It was only a half-hour programme. We concentrated hard and it was quite a relief when everyone was satisfied and it was over. I felt happy and humble at the same time to have my little voice added to the list of those illustrious voices who, through the centuries, had witnessed to Jesus Christ in this wonderful city. My friends in Huddersfield rejoiced with me when I returned.

Chapter 6

Cost of Discipleship

My delightful weekend in Oxford left me feeling exhilarated and excited with the programme Father Bernard had initiated and planned for me. There was no shortage of invitations. As Jesus had promised, He was opening doors for me. I prayed and read my Bible daily, longing to keep close to Him so that as I walked through the doors He opened for me, He would walk with me. It was the only way I knew to ensure that His name and His alone would be glorified.

Waiting for me when I got back to Huddersfield was an invitation from Pastor Samuel in Sheffield, who wanted me to give my testimony and address his congregation. He had arranged for me to meet his people on three occasions – Tuesday, Wednesday and Thursday evenings. The Pastor could not fetch me himself, since he rode a scooter. This presented no problem since I knew that Eric would take me to the bus station and make sure that I got on the right bus. This gradually became the pattern for me as I developed greater and greater confidence in travelling alone. I was beginning to become familiar with coaches and timetables.

I found it relaxing to travel by coach and enjoyed just sitting and admiring the beautiful scenery along the way as the coaches sped along. The smooth rides contrasted sharply with the bumpy ones I used to have in Pakistan. Even better was the fact that there was no standing, no shoving, no argument about whose seat it was, and no confusion. The freedom from annoyance by pedlars selling their wares was also a relief.

Perhaps the biggest difference was the long stretches of silence during a journey. On the buses I was used to in Pakistan people would talk to one another, sometimes at the top of their voices. In England there were only short polite conversations and everyone was so courteous. I also observed that people say 'thank you' to everyone, even to those doing the most menial jobs. In Pakistan to say 'thank you' is the prerogative of the poor! It is their privilege to serve the rich.

I arrived in Sheffield on Monday and spent the evening with the Pastor and his family. He spoke Urdu and this made it easy for us to communicate and for him to act as my interpreter. I listened to him with great admiration. He seemed to have mastered the art of interpretation, by capturing the nuances of the language which created true understanding and conveyed real depth of feeling. But what interested and amused me was to see and hear him on his motorcycle, because it brought back to me some very vivid memories.

I recalled the day when I sat on the pillion of my nephew's motorcycle for the very first time and clung to him for my very life. It gave me the extraordinary feeling of 'flying' through the air. An even more memorable occasion came to mind. I was due to speak at a women's summer camp at Muree, once the very symbol of the British Raj. It had become a centre of great Christian activity with camps and conferences run by various Christian groups from all over Pakistan. I was due to go on the train, my very first ride on a train, to Rawalpindi and from there to go to the camp at Mubarik to which I had been invited as the main speaker.

My nephew had implored me to alter my plans and attend his wedding which had been fixed for the same weekend. Even though my time was very limited I reluctantly agreed to make some adjustments to my travelling plans and go to the wedding in the hope also that it might give me a good opportunity of witnessing to the family. However, my attempt to witness to the truth that Jesus Christ was the Son of God only met with derision. 'Oh, she is mad, leave her alone,' they said and then added unkindly and cruelly, 'She is no relation of ours, don't speak to her.'

Not surprisingly, when the time came for me to go to the bus station, there was no one to take me. My sister wanted me to stay until the following day but that would have meant that I would miss all my connections. I left without saying goodbye and stood alone in the threatening darkness on the road outside her house. I spoke to Jesus: 'Lord, you know my situation. Take care of me and help me reach the bus station on time. I put myself in your hands.' Immediately, the presence of God wrapped itself around me and I felt safe in that dark and lonely place.

Suddenly, I heard the soft purring noise of a motor cycle engine and a headlight coming towards me. It was a rickshaw. Hope entered my heart and I prayed that the man would stop as I waved. Praise God, he did!

'Can you get me to Badani Bagh quickly please? I have to catch the bus which leaves for Rawalpindi.' I didn't stop to think whether it was safe or not. The driver nodded and I got in and we sped through the streets, covering the fifteen miles in record time.

When we arrived, the driver took my case to the Watan Transport Bus Line and put it under a seat in the bus near the front. I never saw his face as he seemed to be hooded and was dressed in a long brown robe. Perhaps he was a Pathan, I thought. When I tried to offer him payment for his service, he turned slightly towards me and said, 'God has sent me to help you. Go in peace.' With that he turned the sleeve of his robe and I saw Patrus (Peter) written in shiny letters on his arm. His eyes shone so brilliantly that I hardly saw his face.

I was filled with awe and marvelled at the goodness of God to me. My relatives had refused to give me a lift to the bus station, saying scornfully, 'We don't want to pollute our car. Ask your Jesus to take you.' I wished I could have told them that I did and he had answered me in this wonderful way. But it would probably not have made any difference. The incident had left a more intriguing question for me. Why Peter? Perhaps I would never know.

Pastor Samuel in Sheffield had hired a school hall for the meetings he arranged. On the first night the hall was filled to capacity and, in good Pentecostal fashion, we had a joyful service, with hearty and lusty singing. Happiness seemed to exude from these lovely Christian people. The reality of Jesus going around and touching and healing people filled the atmosphere. It was no wonder that all eyes were focused upon me as I stood up to give my testimony. My experience was echoed in the hearts and minds of those whose bodies had also been touched by Jesus. But my mind had been on the apostle Peter earlier and suddenly something clicked in me. Jesus had told me to tell his

57

people: '**I am alive and I am coming soon.**' I suddenly realized that this truth was precious to Peter.

Was it not Peter who exhorted the disciples to keep looking to the Lord and waiting faithfully for his return? In 2 Peter 3:2–4, 8–10, it says:

> Beloved, you remember the predictions of the holy prophets and the commandment of the Lord and Saviour through your apostles. First of all you must understand this, that scoffers will come in the last days with scoffing, following their passions and saying, 'Where is the promise of his coming? For ever since the fathers fell asleep, all things have continued as they were from the beginning of creation. But do not ignore this one fact, beloved, that with the Lord, one day is as a thousand years, a thousand years as one day. The Lord is not slow about his promises as some count slowness, but is forbearing toward you, not wishing that any should perish, but that all should reach repentance.

God's forbearance was the real miracle, not my physical healing. I will die one day, but God's gift of eternal life which he is longing to give is the one we should reach out for. That was the gist of my message to those who came to hear me in Sheffield that night.

It had been a long service – up to three hours – but during it I felt upheld. It was as if a girdle of power was around my waist giving me the strength and power to endure. Many came up to me after the service and said, 'This is surely the work of God.' James, the headmaster of the school, was particularly pleased, and said: 'I see that Jesus is bringing in his flock from every nation.' It was strange that he should have echoed the very words that were spoken to me in Oxford. Had Jesus brought me all the way to England from Pakistan to bring in his sheep? It was a wonderful thought. The British Consul in Islamabad had said that missionaries went from England to Pakistan, not the other way round. But here was I, a crippled Muslim girl, raised by Jesus to newness of life, actually being one of His 'missionaries.' How he overturns our earthly notions!

On the last evening, James brought along one of his students to see me after the meeting. He was a sixteen-year-old Muslim student, a fervent follower of Muhammad. His father was with him. They had brought their Quran with them and wanted me to show them the verses in it which referred to Jesus. When I reached out to take hold of the book, they refused to let me touch it. 'You can't touch our Quran. It's a holy book and must not be touched by infidels. You are a Christian now, an infidel, and you must not touch our Quran,' he shouted at me and held it protectively.

I recalled how my own father had treated the Quran. He would take it down from its high shelf, the highest in the room since nothing must be put on or above it. Then he would kiss the green silk cover and recite the Bismillah ('i-Rahman-ir-Raheem' – I begin this in the name of God, the Compassionate, the Merciful). After this he would perform the Wudu (ritual ablutions before touching the book), unwrap the green cover, repeat Bismillah, and then place the Quran on a rail, touching the book only with his fingertips.

That picture softened the rebuff I had just experienced. Gently, I said to father and son. 'Muhammad is my ancestor. How can you say to me that I must not touch his book? Can you forbid the descendant of Muhammad to touch his holy book? My father was a Pir. His name was Shah. My name is still Gulshan Esther Shah. I am not denied the use of his name because I am no longer a Muslim. If you respect Muhammad, as you obviously do, then you should also show respect to his descendant. I belong to Jesus Christ now and Jesus is mentioned in the Quran. Why shouldn't I touch it when Jesus Christ is the one who first directed me to read about him in it?'

I said what came to my mind. My arguments could have been better, but they sufficed. Father and son looked at me, studying me for a while. The father particularly, with his long beard, looked intimidating. In the end they handed me the Quran – but reluctantly. I opened it and found the verses which for three years I had read faithfully. I read them to father and son in Arabic and then invited them to read the verses for themselves.

When they had read the verses, they expressed their feelings in no uncertain terms: 'We believe that Jesus was holy and respect Him. He was probably greater than all the other prophets except Muhammad. But we simply cannot believe that He was the Son of God.' I recognized how hard it was for them to believe this. Was it not also a stumbling block to the Jews who accused Jesus of blasphemy, of daring to put himself on the same level as God?

This father and son before me spoke for all those who are more than ready to accept Jesus as a prophet, a great teacher, a messenger from God, but who find it difficult to accept the truth Jesus taught about himself. I turned to them and said: 'Only God himself can convince us of this truth.' I opened my Bible and found Matthew 16:16, 17 and read the verses to them:

Peter said to Jesus, 'You are the Christ, the Son of

the living God.' Jesus answered, 'Blessed are you,
Simon Barjona! For flesh and blood has not revealed
this to you, but my father who is in heaven.'

This dialogue took place in the hall in front of all
those who had gathered. The pastor translated for
them. The outcome filled us with great joy. The father
said, 'When God showed you this truth you believed.
Now you have shown us. Why shouldn't we also
believe? We can see that Jesus Christ is from God,
that he is greater than all the prophets, in fact he
must be the Son of God.' God's light had begun to
shine in the darkness of their hearts.

I returned home from Sheffield to Huddersfield,
where more invitations awaited me. I was thrilled to
see so many Pakistanis longing to hear the Word of
God. From being just nominal Christians many
turned to the Lord to seek renewed forgiveness and
to dedicate their lives afresh to Him. A growing
understanding was developing inside me as I saw why
Jesus sent me to 'His people' and not to those who
had not heard and responded to his Gospel.

Many of those who came to hear me had been born
in Pakistan and knew how difficult it was to confess
oneself a Christian in the midst of primarily Muslim
areas in Britain without incurring the wrath of the
local Muslims. The way I was treated by my own
family did not come as a surprise to them and they
could empathize with me. A deep and lasting bond
was being forged between us, as together we experienced Jesus working in our midst.

One man who was in hospital with a heart problem
heard of my testimony. He was determined to get to
one of my meetings and left hospital to attend. He
came every night and I prayed for him. On the last

night he came forward joyfully and shared his news. With tears streaming down his face he said: 'On Thursday evening I had a vision and in it I was having an operation. During the operation I saw fat being removed from around my heart. The next day I had X-rays taken, and when the doctors looked at them, they found that there was nothing wrong with my heart. Jesus has healed me completely.' He went away rejoicing in the power and goodness of God.

Another encouraging testimony was given by a lady who had problems with her eyes. She had been attending the eye clinic in a hospital at Huddersfield and had been told by the specialist that within one month she would lose her sight in both eyes. Shattered by this news and with a broken heart she came night after night to our meetings, believing that Jesus could heal her too. Her faith was rewarded. On the last evening, during the prayer session, Jesus touched her and her sight was restored immediately. When she saw her doctor again he found nothing wrong with her eyes. The disease had completely gone.

Inevitably, these signs of his presence and love for us which Jesus was performing in our midst prompted the observation and question: 'Sister Gulshan, it is obvious that Jesus' healing power is flowing through you. Why don't you concentrate on holding healing services? Many non-Christians would become converted and then there will be more of us to witness to his name.'

I had to be on my guard against this kind of temptation. I saw it as only another version of my aunt's interpretation: I was to give alms to the poor. The story of Jesus' temptation in the wilderness was always a great comfort to me on such occasions. Had he not also been tempted to do that which would draw the crowd – to turn stones into bread to satisfy human need. But his answer: 'Man shall not live by bread alone, but by every word that proceeds from the mouth of God' (Matthew 4:4), guided me and greatly strengthened me in my resolve to make it my priority to deliver the message he had given me – the message of his salvation – and to remind his people that he would be coming soon.

On 1st November I went to meet a group of Muslim women in a school room in Bradford. These were women who had not been long in England. There was no problem with communication since they all spoke either Urdu or Punjabi. I gave them a brief version of my encounters with Jesus Christ and of the miraculous way he had healed me. Then it was time for discussion. They asked me a few questions about my new faith but inevitably the implications of forsaking Islam for Christianity took up the rest of our morning.

One of the women said to me: 'Sister, I respect you and I understand what you are trying to say. But I am afraid to believe in Jesus Christ because I know what will happen when my husband or my father or even my brother finds out. They would despise me for becoming a Christian. I might even be cast out of my own home. What will happen then? When this occurs in Pakistan, it is very difficult for a woman. If it should happen here in Bradford, it would be disastrous. I could not face it.' My heart went out to her. I knew exactly what she was talking about and what she was feeling. The others began one after the other to open up.

'We have only recently come to join our husbands. Many of them have been over here on their own for a long time. They would not bring us over until they had got good jobs and earned enough money to share a house or buy one of their own. How could we possibly think of giving up Islam? If we did we would destroy these homes that our husbands worked so hard and so long to secure for us. You would not want us to harm them or hurt them, would you?'

'Yes,' another added. 'If we could speak English it would not be so bad. We could perhaps find jobs to support ourselves.'

This brought forth the retort: 'And what about our children? What would become of them? You know how it is. Now that we are are all together again our lives are beginning to look as if we have never left Pakistan. We have close ties with our uncles and aunts and their children. We help and support each other. What you are asking us to do is to break up our families and we cannot do this.'

The sad tale continued. 'Soon our children will be old enough for us to think of marriage partners for them. We cannot afford to go to Pakistan each time we want a husband or a wife for our daughters and sons. We have to maintain good relations within our community. We must all stick together. There is too much at stake.'

I decided to share my own experiences that I had had with my family. I told them that after I left home and worked at the Sunrise School for the Blind, I still wanted to retain a good relationship with my family. I had phoned my younger brother Alim Shah. 'I thought I should let you know that I have become a Christian.'

He was shocked. 'What have you done?' he asked. 'Return home straight away and forget all this nonsense.'

I responded: 'How can I forget? I have found Jesus, the Way, the Truth and the Life.'

'Have you gone quite mad?' he asked angrily. 'If you keep on saying this to me my door will be shut to you forever. As far as I am concerned, you are dead!'

My audience gasped as I continued to relate my conversation with my brother: 'How can I give up the truth now I have it?' I asked.

He said grimly: 'In that case, my door is shut to you. You are dead! I never want to see your face again and you will never see mine.' With that, he banged down the phone.

The women looked at one another. They did not have to speak. Each one knew what the other was thinking: If that happened to me what would I do? They asked me to carry on with the story of my persecution, and so I returned to my account.

'That same day I decided to come out into the open and tell the whole family that I was now a Christian. My elder brother's reaction was not unexpected. He wrote to me: "My dear. You used to love Allah very much and my father used to love you. You learnt a lot about Islam from him. You must know that a daughter of a Sayed cannot go the way you are going. You must turn back. Alim has told me that you now believe that Jesus is the Son of God. This is not right for our family or for our religion. You must come back to my house and listen to my advice. As you know, I have the deeds to all your property. You cannot claim your property now you are a Christian. If you do not leave Christianity, I may have to kill you. You know that my religion allows me to kill a sister who has become a Christian and afterwards still to go to Paradise." '

My story seemed to confirm their worst fears. 'We could not endure all that,' they said.

I looked at them directly and said, 'If in your heart you receive Jesus Christ as your Lord and Saviour he will give you strength and courage to face even worse persecution. He is faithful and keeps his promise to his followers.'

Then they said to me, 'We too will pray for Jesus to come into our hearts as you did for three long years. If he appears to us as he did to you, then we will believe.'

Chapter 7

The Christian Family

My witnessing was taking on a whirlwind appearance. No sooner was I finished with one set of engagements when another was arranged for me. I thanked my Lord that I never wavered or faltered but that His power upheld me. Knowing the source of my strength added to my stamina.

On Wednesday 3rd November I returned to Huddersfield but not for long. Within two days I was on the road again. This time it was to London. Eric took me to the bus station where I got a coach to London. Unlike the time when I was fourteen years of age and in my wheelchair confined to our bedroom with my two maids, I was free to go wherever I pleased. As the coach neared London, I was thrilled to be going to this great capital city of which I had heard so much. Later I had an opportunity to see parts of London by car.

Pastor Daniel Singh, who had invited me, was in charge of an Asian congregation, which consisted mainly of Pakistani Christians. The Pastor himself was from a Sikh family. I was not surprised to see that he was not wearing a turban with his long hair wrapped in it, or carrying a comb or a dagger. As he explained to me: 'We have exchanged these for the cross of Jesus Christ. We no longer bear the marks of allegiance to the teachings of Guru Nanak and the Granth Sahib. Instead we have put on the armour of God – a girdle of truth, the breastplate of righteousness, the Gospel of peace on our feet, the shield of faith, the helmet of salvation, and the sword of the Spirit.'

I met his lovely family who were all Christians. With Sikhs, it is usual for whole families to be converted rather than individuals within the family. Consequently, relationships tend to be warm and friendly and the women seem to be more relaxed and secure since they are not expected to be as submissive to their husbands as Muslim women.

On 18th November I was taken to Bedford where I stayed for three days. The church which had invited me and whose elder had fetched me was a Methodist church with an English pastor. The congregation was made up mainly of Indians. I was familiar with the Methodist church since the first church I attended in Pakistan after my conversion was the Warris Street Methodist in Lahore. It was there that I first experienced the joy of Christian fellowship.

It had been arranged that I should have house meetings on Thursday, Friday and Saturday evenings, with different groups of people. Sometimes there were Muslims among them. One evening after the meeting a Muslim man asked me: 'How can you live with Christian people? You were not brought up in a Christian home and for most of your life you lived among Muslim people.'

He asked this in a very friendly manner and not in the usual aggressive manner I had come to expect from Muslims, especially the men. He seemed to be genuinely interested to know how I coped with the changes which have inevitably accompanied my conversion to Christianity. I welcomed the opportunity to explain how I felt and what principles guided me. So I said to him: 'The biggest change was that which took place within me and not in my outward circum-

stances. In the New Testament it says, "If anyone is
in Christ, he is a new creation; the old has passed
away, behold the new has come." '

I continued to explain to him that in Jesus Christ
I became a new person with new allegiances and new
feelings of love and brotherhood. 'I am now united in
love in Christ Jesus and because other Christians are
also united in Him, we are united together. His love
binds us together and we grow in love for Him and
for one another daily. Other Christians are now my
brothers and sisters. In Jesus Christ we have become
a new family.

'When Jesus appeared to me he had said, "My
people are your people," and he continually reminds
me of this wonderful truth. His people are my people.
Therefore, I love them even as I love Jesus himself.
There is no difficulty in living with people who are
my own and who I love as if they were my own flesh
and blood.'

All this talk about loving one another did not seem
to impress him, as his next question clearly indicated.
'Have you thought that Christians may hate you secretly even if you don't hate them?'

'What do you mean?' I asked. 'I have done nothing
to harm anyone. Why should they hate me?'

'Well, you claim that Jesus himself touched you and
healed your crippled body. Many of them cannot
make such a claim.'

I was beginning to understand what he was trying
to say. 'You mean they are jealous of me and hate me
as a result. But even if they are jealous, and I don't
believe they are, the only thing they could want
would be for Jesus to do the same for them whether
they are crippled in body, mind or spirit.'

'Yes, but it is not only that. You are a Pakistani, a

former Muslim. Many Europeans think that Christianity is their religion. By saying that Jesus loves you you are taking a love that is theirs.'

How great was his misunderstanding of Christianity!

'Christianity is for everyone. God loves the world and not just any one nation. Jesus died for all.' And I quoted St. Paul: 'There is neither Jew nor Greek, there is neither slave nor free, there is neither male nor female; for you are all one in Christ Jesus.' (Galatians 3:28).

My questioner did not give up easily and I was glad, because our Asian audience was enjoying this discussion. His next question was: 'How can you, who have been brought up in Purdah, sit with men in the congregation? You know that Muslim women are not allowed in the mosque. They say their prayers at home. Shouldn't you do the same?'

Muslim men especially cannot understand how age-long traditions concerning the respective places of men and women, whether in the home or in the place of worship, can be flagrantly disregarded. The demarcation lines between men and women in Islam, whether they stem from the Quran itself or from tradition, have almost divine sanction. I did not find it easy to answer him. A simplistic answer would create more misunderstanding and the occasion was not right for a very detailed one.

So I said to him: 'God deals with each one of us individually. When we meet to worship Him we relate in the first place to Him. He occupies our thoughts and engages our minds and hearts. Our love and relationship to one another flows out of this first relationship. In our act of worship together, God's Holy Spirit is present in our midst and He cleanses us from all unworthy and sinful thoughts so that we can worship God in holiness and purity. We become the family of God worshipping our heavenly Father.'

I am sorry to say that he was only baffled by such ideas. He had no concept of the Holy Spirit. If I had said that we had used water to wash ourselves and prepare ourselves for prayer he would more easily have understood. He summed up his feelings very clearly when he said: 'All this makes no sense whatever to me. Only Christians can understand them.'

I understood and felt much sympathy for his position. To draw a line between religion and culture is not easy. It takes a whole lifetime to work out all the changes and adjustments one must make. I am relieved to know that God is more concerned with what is in our hearts rather than what is in our outward appearance or actions. I still wear my Pakistani dress. I like Pakistani food and I enjoy listening to psalms and hymns sung in Urdu. But the meaning and purpose of life, my hope for the future, and the values I seek to uphold and live by are Christian. It is when it comes to traditional customs and habits that it is not always easy to determine where to draw the line.

The hectic pace of my ministry kept up its momentum. Two days after I returned to Huddersfield, I had three successive nights of services in Halifax. These were to be in the Elim Pentecostal church and as most of the congregation were English, Eric translated for me.

At the end of one of these services, a lady stood up in the congregation and boldly declared: 'Today, my vision has come true. Sister Gulshan has come from God to us.' Every one in the congregation turned

71

towards her, wondering to what vision she was referring and waited expectantly for some explanation.

She obliged: 'In August 1982, before Sister Gulshan ever came to this country, I saw her in my vision. I had been praying one night and after praying I had a vision. In it I saw her dressed in her white coat, and wearing dark glasses. In the vision Jesus said to me: "This is my messenger to my sheep." She looked at me. Jesus also told me her full name but afterwards I could only remember Esther.' And turning to me she added: 'Since then I have been longing to meet you. So you see, my vision has come true today.'

The whole congregation rejoiced with this lady because of her wonderful experience, and especially because of her revelation that Jesus himself had brought me here. This is not the first time that I was told that I was being used to bring in his sheep. The way she linked my Christian name Esther with this work fascinated me. Was my name more significant than I realized? I recalled that at my baptism, the four pastors present had a list of names from which to choose mine. After praying for guidance all four chose Esther. I told the Halifax congregation that my Christian name had not been my choice or the people's, but God's.

Later when I was on my own I was prompted to find the story of Esther in the Bible and read it again. It is a lovely story.

When Queen Vashti disobeyed her husband, King Ahasuerus of the Persians, she was removed and the King sought another Queen. A Jew named Mordecai, who had raised his niece Esther, introduced her to the king. She was very beautiful and immediately he fell in love with her and made her his Queen, giving her the best rooms in the palace. He did not know that she was a Jewess.

Later a decree was issued that all the Jews be destroyed, and Haman was put in charge of the operation. Mordecai implored Esther to tell the King that she was Jewess but Esther was afraid. She was sure she would not be spared. She told Mordecai to gather all the Jews in the city and command them to fast for three days and three nights. She and her hand-maidens would also fast.

On the third day she dressed in all her fine robes. The King was so pleased with her that he said, 'Whatever you want I will give you.' So she said to him, 'If it pleases my lord, let my life and the lives of my people be spared. I am a Jewess. My people have been sold and now we are all to be destroyed.' The king was outraged and he ordered Haman to be hanged. Mordecai was put in his place, the Jews were delivered and rejoiced. Many who were not Jews became Jews for the first time.

This delightful story thrilled me. I too was being used to deliver God's people, only not from physical death, but from darkness into the glorious light of the Gospel of Jesus Christ. I felt so unworthy to be so used but it was to the glory of God and to his name be praise forever. His name was further glorified as he confirmed my testimony and my message concerning Jesus Christ by signs of healing of body and of soul.

I needed a break and Father Bernard provided this for me by taking Elizabeth and me in his black Austin mini to the Community of the Resurrection at Mirfield. We attended the service in the chapel and after it Father Bernard introduced me to the brothers and fathers who were most interested to learn of my ministry in England. We bought a few gifts from the shop for our friends and relatives in Pakistan.

Once again I was privileged to make another visit to London. This time it was to Southall where a large number of Sikhs had chosen to make their new home. Many had come from the Punjab where, in the last century and early in the twentieth century, missionaries had been successful in taking the Gospel of God concerning Jesus to the followers of Guru Nanak. In the Punjab some of them had been Roman Catholics, Methodists and Pentecostals, but here they worshipped together and called themselves the Asian church.

To my surprise when I arrived there was distinct coldness on the part of the Christians. There was no warmth or affection such as I had had in the other places I visited. I felt strange as if I did not belong there. I was sure that it was not because I was a converted Muslim and not a converted Sikh. The cause seemed to go deeper than that. I began to wonder whether my ministry would be effective among such people, but I could not just pack my bags and return home to Huddersfield. That would have meant admitting defeat. I committed my fears to the Lord in prayer.

It became clear to me later that the underlying reason for the strained atmosphere was the gentleman in whose home I was a guest. Many in the congregation disliked him because they said that he was not a good man. One of them even said to me, 'you should have known what kind of person he is before you accepted his invitation.' I was deeply distressed by this. I had no means of checking out the man before I agreed to come. Besides, I asked myself, what difference would it have made?

I marvelled at how the experiences of Jesus Christ

kept repeating themselves in my humble life. Matthew 9:10–13 came into my mind:

> And as he sat at table in the home, behold, many tax collectors and sinners came and sat down with Jesus and his disciples. And when the Pharisees saw this, they said to his disciples: 'Why does your teacher eat with tax collectors and sinners?' When Jesus heard this he said, 'Those who are well have no need of a physician, but those who are sick . . . I came not to call the righteous but sinners.'

I found great comfort in this passage while I contemplated what to do in this very difficult situation in which I unwittingly found myself.

I came to the conclusion that somehow I would have to explain to those who felt offended by my presence in the gentleman's house that this fact should not be allowed to hinder their response to the message Jesus had given me for his people. So I said to them as kindly as I could: 'I am a servant of God. The whole world is God's world. I go wherever he leads me. Whenever and wherever Jesus sends me I go, and I never question his will for me. My home is in heaven and my dependence is upon God only. If he chooses for me to stay in this man's house then that is where I will stay.'

These words seemed to soften their attitude and I managed to persuade them to allow the Holy Spirit, and not their own likes and dislikes to guide them. In the end, I committed them into the hands of Jesus and returned to Huddersfield in the hope that eventually there would be some fruit from my labours in the Lord's vineyard.

Chapter 8

Christmas in Oxford

I had been in England for nearly three months. Places I had never heard of had become firmly fixed in my mind. Well, not so much the places, but the Christian people in those places. I had certainly toured the country, but had not seen its historic places or its fine buildings. It had been a constant giving of myself to the task I had been commissioned to do. This had involved me in doing just what my uncle had advised me not to do when he said to me soon after my miraculous healing: 'Listen Gulshan. I am speaking to you now as if I were your father. Whatever Jesus wants, you give it to him – land or money, but don't leave your country or your religion and don't give yourself.' I am glad he wasn't my real father!

But respite was at hand. I had been invited by the Asian Christians in Oxford to spend Christmas with them. I looked forward to it as a time of refreshment and rest. What better season could I have chosen than this one when we remember and celebrate the coming into the world of the Son of God. For me He was not just the babe of Bethlehem but my living Lord and Saviour.

It had been arranged that I would be the guest of the pastor and his family. This plan was changed shortly before I arrived. Susan explained to me later, 'Before you came, the pastor came to see my father, an elder in the church, to ask if you could come and stay with us. He said that he did not have a heater in his guest room, and wondered if you could stay in my room. I was so pleased when I heard this because I was looking forward to your coming.'

When I arrived in Oxford, Susan and her brother met me at the station and drove me to their home. The city of dreaming spires took on an ethereal look as lights twinkled from the trees, and the lines strung across the streets and the colourful decorations swayed in the gentle breeze. The beautiful sounds of Christmas music pervaded the air and filled my soul with longing for the heavenly realm where the choir sings 'Hallelujah to the Lamb who was slain and who is alive forever', as in my vision.

For the moment, however, I had to settle for a more humble abode. My host lived in a modest semi-detached house with his wife, his two sons and his only daughter Susan, and a nephew. It was a warm and comfortable home with a feeling of 'home from home' for me. I was powerfully reminded of my own adopted family from whom I was separated for the first time at Christmas. I could not let my thoughts linger on them for too long without sadness creeping into my heart.

Mr and Mrs Christopher were very kind and welcoming. 'It is a blessing to have you with us,' they said as they made every effort to make me feel at home in their midst. There was no language barrier between us. They spoke Punjabi. He had been a cook in the British army in India and when the Major for whom he worked retired and came to England, he brought Mr Christopher over, with two of his sons. Another son joined him later. Once he had got himself established, his wife, with two other sons and Susan applied for a visa but she was refused several times. Each time she applied she was told, 'These children are your neighbour's children. We cannot allow you to take them with you.'

Susan remembered those difficult days. 'My mother used to get so angry. She was a Christian woman, brought up in a Christian family, and telling the truth was one thing which had been drummed into her from childhood. Now she found herself confronted with people who called her a liar to her face. She used to get deeply hurt and each time she would say to the authorities "Why should I lie about my children? If these were my neighbours' children I could easily give them back to their parents so that I could be free to join my husband." It took her six long frustrating years to obtain a visa for us. In the end my eldest brother decided to remain in India.'

Now here they were, well settled and getting ready to join in the festivities of this joyful season. In one corner of their living room was a modest-sized Christmas tree with beautifully wrapped gifts underneath it. Every weekend from the beginning of December to Christmas Eve, choirs of various Asian congregations would visit each other's towns for fellowship. Sometimes they would hire a van to transport themselves and their instruments. Susan and her brother were in the choir of the Oxford congregation and went out carol singing every night.

I was not aware at the time that this meeting with Susan had a special significance for her, and that it would eventually for me also. Let her tell her story in her own words:

'My brother and I returned from our carol singing late on that first night that Sister Gulshan came to stay with us. When I went to my room she was already fast asleep. As usual I got into my bed and prayed.

'Now for many years my one special prayer had been that the Lord would send a woman with whom I could go about preaching the Gospel. I had given my life to the Lord as a young girl of twelve. The memory of that evening when I made my commitment has never dimmed in my mind.

'We were at a service at the Elim Pentecostal Church when the preacher invited those who wanted to commit themselves to the celibate life to stand up. Now this in itself was unusual since one does not associate the call to celibacy with Pentecostals. How strange are the ways of our God! I cannot explain what it was that made me do it but I stood up boldly.

'The leader of the choir who was sitting next to me was as dumb-founded as the rest of the congregation. She kept pulling my dress to make me sit down. She was sure that I could not possibly know what I was doing. I must confess that even now I cannot remember what was going through my mind. All I was aware of was that I did not want to marry. I wanted to give my life to Jesus Christ in this way.

'The next morning when we went visiting from door to door the choir leader's mind was distracted by the event of the previous night. She tried to persuade me not to take my commitment seriously. Such an act was foolish she said and could be disastrous for a girl of twelve. However, I stood my ground. There might be other ways of giving oneself to Jesus Christ, but this was the way I had chosen and I was determined to keep my promise.

'My mother was very pleased with my commitment. She was a deeply religious woman who prayed regularly for two hours at a time. She had taught us to pray and made sure that we went to church every Sunday even when she herself could not go. We were a poor family in the Punjab and mother had to fetch the grass for our cow which she could only do when the service was on. This used to upset her and when she came to England she never missed a service.

'The only conditions she laid down, however, was that the person with whom I chose to share in the Lord's work had to be a woman of whom she approved. From then on I prayed earnestly, asking the Lord to send me such a person – someone who was close to him, someone who was strong in the faith and who could also strengthen me when my faith wavered.

'The Lord answered my prayer in a wonderful way, but it took me some time to understand the full significance of his answer. Since my commitment, I had often seen in visions a person standing before me – a person dressed all in white. Because the face was always unclear, I presumed that it was the Lord Jesus Christ. I took it to mean that this was his way of reassuring me that he was with me.

'However, when I went to sleep that first night Sister Gulshan was in my room, I had the same vision again but this time it was accompanied by a voice saying to me, "This is not me but Gulshan Esther, for whom you have been waiting. Your prayer has been answered. From now on you will witness to me with Gulshan Esther."

'I woke up, got up from my bed and went over to Sister Gulshan's bed, partly hoping to find that she also had had a vision or a word from the Lord but she was fast asleep! Then I recalled that she wore white when I first met her and yet strangely that had not registered in my mind at the time. Only now, as I looked down upon her, did I recognize her as the person in my vision. I was ecstatic with joy and just could not go back to sleep. The whole course of my life was about to change and I was filled with excitement.

'The next morning I could hardly wait to tell my mother. I rushed downstairs to find her. I found her in the kitchen preparing breakfast. "Mother," I blurted out, "I had a vision last night and in it was Sister Gulshan. I also heard the voice of Jesus saying that she was the person with whom I was to do the Lord's work. Isn't this wonderful news?"

'To my amazement, mother told me that she too had had a similar vision and Jesus had said to her, "Give your daughter to Gulshan Esther so that they could work together for my glory."

' "Oh Susan," she said, "I am so happy that both of us have had this clear direction from the Lord. You must do as he has directed." '

I feel humbled and gratified by Susan's testimony.

With such a blessing from her mother, Susan was confirmed in her resolution to serve Jesus in this way. The whole family was pleased with this development and thanked God for the way he was going to use the family. Susan's brother often translated for me in the services. Thus it was that Jesus provided a companion for me. His goodness overwhelmed me. He had sent his disciples out in twos and now he was doing the same for me. He knew my need even before I was aware of it or asked him to satisfy it.

Christmas was a busy time for the household as friends and relatives dropped in for a chat, laden with their expensive presents. I could not help noticing that our Asian friends did not economize when it came to buying presents for another. The ladies excelled themselves in their dress and jewellery. It was not uncommon to see them in one beautiful sari in the morning and another in the evening. They had parties on Christmas Eve which went into the early hours of the morning.

Christmas Day was a very special day for me in more senses than one. It was the day when my interview would be broadcast on Radio Oxford and I was eagerly looking forward to it. At 4.00 p.m. we were all gathered round the radio and waited. The interview came across well and I was thrilled to know that I had been able to make this act of witness to Jesus. He who had been born nearly two thousand years ago was alive and he wanted me to remind his people of this great truth which should be at the heart of the Christian festivities.

I was very pleased with the way my ministry in England had worked out. Addressing large groups of people did not seem to make me nervous in any way, as I was not seeking to exalt myself but to glorify Jesus Christ. What gave me even greater pleasure, however, was to meet individual people who had been touched by my message to turn anew to the Lord.

One such was to become my friend. She is a very shy lady called Nina who has to summon up a lot of courage to make any public statement. She had heard my testimony on tape and came to the Christmas Eve service at which I was speaking. This was the first time she had seen me and she kept thinking, 'How can I speak to Sister Gulshan?' She met me after the service but somehow could not bring herself to say much to me. She returned the next day for the Christmas Day service and this time she resolved that she would invite me to her home. I said to her, 'When it is the Lord's will I will come to your house.' That must have seemed a cold response to her but she did not give up. Such was her determination.

Nina had been born into a Christian family. She and her husband, both nominal Christians, came to England from the Punjab with their first son, George. Three other children have been born to them since. Their church-going was limited to occasional Sundays and always at Christmas and Easter.

After the birth of her children, Nina developed severe asthma. In 1981 she had such bad attacks that she thought she might die. She could neither do housework nor look after her husband and children very well. She could do no cooking. For three months she saw a doctor privately in Birmingham but she did not improve. Sleeping became difficult and she had an odd feeling of some obstruction in her throat. When she began to vomit blood if was feared that she might have cancer. The threat of dying and leaving her children greatly troubled her.

One night at one o'clock when the rest of the family were asleep she had a most frightening experience. She described it to me.

'My body became very cold, my heart was beating unusually fast, and I felt as if something came out of my body and flew away. I felt a strong urge to pray and to read the Bible. This was new to me because I had never really prayed and since I had not gone to school in India I could not read. Still I prayed in my heart, "O God, if it is your will, take me but look after my children."

'George, my son, woke up and realized that something was wrong. My husband was on night shift. I asked George to phone the doctor but for some strange reason he could not find the telephone. I asked for my Bible and tried to read it. I found it hard to understand but the wonderful thing was I could read it – I, who had never read before. I said to George, "Something is happening to me. As I read, my body is getting warmer and warmer as if a new life is flowing into me." Poor George did not know what to make of this. After reading and praying I fell asleep.

'My husband was very concerned when he came home in the morning and I told him what had happened. He asked his niece to sleep with me the following night, but the experience was not repeated. I knew in my heart that it wouldn't. But something else happened.

'One day while I was lying on the bed I saw in the dressing table mirror in front of the bed two persons sitting on either side of the bed and there was one on the middle behind me but slightly to the side. His eyes shone so brilliantly that I could not see his face. I could not tell whether it was a man or a woman. Great joy and peace flooded my whole being. I prayed for help to read the Bible and gradually I have been able to read it. I began to feel physically better from that moment.'

Such was her story. I did visit Nina shortly after the Christmas Day service. She was by now convinced that she should repent of her sins and give her life to the Lord. We had a Bible study which I led and after it, when everyone had gone, she asked, 'Please tell me what to do. I want to give my life to Jesus.'

We prayed together and she accepted anew Jesus Christ as her Saviour. I also prayed about her asthma. When she next saw her doctor he told her that she needed no more prescriptions. Her asthma had gone. She also went to the hospital four times to have blood tests to see whether she had cancer. All these proved negative. She has had excellent health since then.

With ten others, six of them Asians, she was baptized in the Elim Pentecostal Church.

Among these were Aman Jeet, his wife Krishna and Krishna's mother. It was through Susan that I met this wonderful family. Susan was working with Krishna in Pembroke College and one day, Krishna shared a problem that was weighing heavily on her mind. 'I wish we could do something for Deep,' as she fondly referred to her younger brother. 'He has kidney failure and is on the waiting list for a transplant operation. He is losing all his hair.'

Now for a Sikh to lose his hair is a real tragedy. The sight of it all neatly wrapped up in a turban speaks clearly of a man whose beliefs are important to him. This may bring him into conflict with the law as, for example, when it became law in England for all those who ride motor cycles to wear helmets. Sikhs were torn between obeying the law of their adopted country and obeying the rule of their religion.

Krishna went on to tell Susan: 'Unless a donor is found soon, he will die. We are at the mercy of circumstances. There is nothing we can do.' With a sense of hopelessness she burst into tears, and accused Susan of keeping me to herself. Susan was deeply moved and promised that she would ask me to pray for Deep.

A meeting was promptly arranged, and fervent prayers were offered for Deep. His mother, although a Sikh, was desperate to clutch anything which held hope for her son. She invited me to her home together with Aman Jeet and his wife Krishna. She implored me, 'Please pray for my son. You are our only hope.'

The family sat quietly while I prayed my Christian prayers and asked Jesus to meet both their physical and spiritual needs. Two weeks later we saw the answer to our prayers. Due to an unfortunate accident, an eight-year-old girl was killed in an accident, and her sad and grieving parents gave permission for her organs to be used for transplantation. Deep was operated upon successfully and after a few weeks had recovered fully. The only shadow over our joy to this answer to prayer was the tragic circumstance which made the transplantation possible.

Deep's deliverance convinced the whole family of the truth I was anxious for them to hear, that Jesus is the Way, the Truth, and the Life. Their holy book is now the Bible which they still study with great enthusiasm. Deep's mother is now a fine Christian lady who manages to strengthen the faith of her whole family.

Aman Jeet's own testimony warms my heart. He had resisted the Lord for a long time. As he said to me, 'Before I met you I had no interest in the Bible. I was a Sikh and a faithful follower of Guru. . . . I carried his photograph with me everywhere and even insisted that Krishna should repeat some of his sayings although I knew that she was a Christian. This had created a great conflict within her as you know and for ten years she prayed for me without any answer.

'Matters came to a head when with our two children we went to India. She saw my guru with six or seven of his disciples dressed in all their paraphernalia and blowing trumpets as they walked through the streets. The sight disgusted her because she saw clearly for the first time that I was worshipping a man and not a God. She then realized that her prayers for me had not been answered because unwittingly she had been worshipping two gods and serving two masters.

'She determined from that day that she would be a faithful Christian and the Holy Spirit revealed to her that if she loved me she would speak to me about Jesus Christ. It was around this time that she met Susan who told her about you. She longed to share her problem with someone, and you seemed just the right person. Through her persistence I was eventually introduced to you. Only after hearing your testimony was I ready to accept Jesus Christ as my Saviour. You remember how you threw the picture of my guru into the river? That was really the end of him for me. I felt liberated at last.

'On the 30th April 1983 when I emerged from the baptismal font my body felt so light: it was as if something had departed from me. That same night I began to read my Bible with enthusiasm and did not want to put it down. My knowledge increased tremendously within a very short time and I began to think that I should work for the Lord. This was why I was so keen to accompany you on your travels.

'I committed this growing awareness to the Lord and continued to witness to him at work, and even after work. On 1st December, around 5.00 a.m., I had a vision in which the Lord spoke to me, "Go and preach the Gospel because the time is near." I asked him, "How can I do that? People will not listen to me." But I was told again, "You take the word and preach. I will judge other people. Don't worry. I am with you. Don't be afraid."

'Since that vision I have drawn closer to the Lord and I am now wholly dependent upon him. Now the whole family go to the Methodist church in Cowley Road. While the pastor is away I take the services. Basically, my message is very simple: "Repent of your sins. The time is near. Believe in Jesus Christ." When I say such things at work, some listen but others scoff.

I take comfort from the fact that Noah had the same response when he preached to his generation and warned them about the coming flood.

'God has blessed me richly with a lovely family of two boys, good health, and I even own two houses. But my burning desire is to live for the glory of Jesus Christ. If he calls me into full time service I am ready. In the meantime I join with my wife in sending Christian literature wherever it is needed. We send free of charge whatever is requested here in England and also abroad. Maybe this is one way in which I am "preaching" his word. I don't know. I leave it in his hands.'

Chapter 9

Media Contacts

Proverbs 16:9, 10.   A man's mind plans his way,
                     But the Lord directs his steps.

What great wisdom is enshrined in those words! On
my arrival at Heathrow airport in September 1982 I
had boldly asked for my six months visa to be changed
to one for only three months. I was confident that in
three months time I would have fulfilled my commission to give the Lord's message to his people.
The hectic pace at which I had lived and given my
testimony during this period seemed to confirm this
expectation. I felt I could say: 'The time of my departure has come. I have fulfilled my task.'

I had spent a happy Christmas. I felt rested and
refreshed. In two weeks time I expected to be on my
way home. My children would be delighted. In their
recent letters, they had pleaded with me. 'Ma-ji,
please come home. We miss you so much. We want
you back here with us. Tell us when you are coming
home.'

I longed to see them again, to hear the familiar
sounds and see the familiar sights again, even to feel
the tropical heat! The winter of 1982 was comparatively mild but I longed for the cool and beautiful
mornings in Pakistan. Yes, I thought, it would be good
to wake up to the sound of tropical birds again.

I had been invited to go up to London again by
Pastor David Singh for two weeks to give my testi-

mony and message. This pleased me because it meant
that up to the last minute I would be giving my Lord's
message to his people. At the end of the two weeks
my time in England would be up. This was not the
first time I thought I could see clearly the end of my
ministry. I recalled how I had come to the same
conclusion in Pakistan.

After obtaining my Bible through the direction
Jesus had given to me in a vision, I had read it and
decided that my next step was to be baptized. I had
said to myself: I have witnessed to Jesus. I have told
the man who gave me the New Testament of my
encounters with Jesus Christ. I have done what Jesus
required. I can be baptized and then go back home
and carry on as normal. But to my surprise, baptism
turned out to be the beginning and not the end of a
new road for me to walk on.

How easily one forgets. In my mind it had all been
neatly worked out. But as the prophet Isaiah says,

> My thoughts are not your thoughts,
> Neither are your ways my ways, says the Lord.

My God had other plans for me. Once again he used
his servants Eric and Father Bernard to direct my
steps. Before I went to Oxford for Christmas, Aramneet Lall had rung me to invite me to London for
a series of meetings. I had reluctantly declined his
invitation saying that my visa expired soon after
Christmas and I would not be able to stay in England.
Unknown to me he rang Father Bernard and Eric
and asked them to try and get my visa extended
adding, 'If you can't, then I will.'

My passport had been kept by Father Bernard. He
was very positive in his reply, 'You do not worry. Go
ahead and plan a programme for Sister Gulshan. I

will see to everything.' Eric, Father Bernard and I spent a long time praying and seeking Jesus' direction. At the end, Father Bernard said to me. 'Sister Gulshan, leave it all in God's hands. Don't think about Pakistan. Go to Oxford for Christmas and afterwards you plan to go to London.'

I was content to do this. But there was a touch of sadness for me. Every two or three weeks, letters had been arriving from friends in Lahore, Faisalabad, and Karachi, pleading with me to return home. However, I was in my Father's hands and that was where I wanted to stay.

After Christmas, Father Bernard phoned to let me know that my visa had been extended for another six months. We all saw God's hands in this and accepted that it was his will that I should continue my ministry in England.

Aramneet Lall was delighted. He said to me, 'The Lord has many more doors to open for you.' I wrote to my children in Pakistan, feeling sad for their sakes. 'I am very sorry I can't return now. I am busy with the Lord's work. But please pray that God will give me time to come and see you soon.'

Mr Lall's words turned out to be prophetic, for door after door began to open for me. And they were not ordinary ones. I was scheduled to address a group of Pakistani and Indian Christians on 2nd January 1983. During the service a video was made. I was unaware of it at the time but later when I saw it, I could hardly believe my eyes. I, Gulshan Esther, who as a Muslim had never had my photograph taken, was now on film talking about what Jesus had done for me. It was truly wonderful. Even in my absence hundreds could now see as well as hear me.

During my time in London, I stayed with Aramneet's family. Aramneet was an elder in the Asian church. I addressed the congregation on two Sundays and during the week we had evening meetings each day in different homes, where twenty-five to thirty people would gather to hear the Lord's word. The Lord confirmed his message with power.

For example, Anand who had had stomach pains for the past ten years asked me to pray for him. I did, and his pains disappeared. Then there was Sheila who for twenty years had suffered from severe back pains. The doctors had given up hope of finding a cure for her, and it was not possible for medical reasons to carry out an operation. Once again the Lord performed a miracle in our presence, for after praying for her she was delivered by Jesus from her pains. These miracles or signs provided his people with the concrete 'evidence' they needed to convince them of the truth of his word. Asian Christians particularly find them useful in their witness to the Lord since their lack of knowledge of the Bible and of God's dealings with his people can be a real hindrance. They can always point to the signs and say with conviction, 'This is what the Lord has done for me. He can do the same for you.'

From London I was taken by James, a Christian brother and elder, to his church in Bedford. I had once before visited Bedford. I was very pleased to have another opportunity to visit those homes I had missed on my first visit. I was even more delighted to find that the Muslim who had refused to let me touch his Quran was now telling others of the salvation which Jesus had offered to him, and offers to all.

Among these were two Muslim ladies who asked me, 'Aren't you fed up with Christian people? Don't you miss your home in Pakistan?' How hard it is for non-Christian people to understand that Jesus tears away the veil which separates people of different nations, enabling them to unite together in Christian love and fellowship. What could I say but reiterate what I have always said: 'Of course, I miss my home in Pakistan but I love Jesus more than I love my home, and I love his people here. How can I be fed up with them?'

It was not always easy to explain that my one and only desire was to be where Jesus wanted me, and that loyalty to him must take precedence in my life over all else. Peter's words to Jesus and Jesus' reply gave me great comfort:

> 'Lo, we have left everything and followed you.' Jesus replied: 'Truly, I say to you, there is no one who has left house, or brothers, or sisters, or mother or father, or children or lands, for my sake and for the Gospel who will not receive a hundredfold now in this time, houses, and brothers, and sisters and mothers and children and lands, and in the age to come eternal life. (Mark 10:28–30; Luke 18:28–30)

Such promises strengthened me as I continued my ministry among his people despite the occasional dark cloud as when, for example, with grave suspicion I was asked, 'Are you trying to become a British citizen?' This hurt me deeply. It was the last thing on my mind. I had no desire to stay in England longer than I needed to. Jesus was in control of my life and he would decide how long I should stay there. I recognized, however, that there was no animosity behind the question. It was not unknown for people to claim to be converted to Christianity in order to gain the support of English Christians in their efforts to become British citizens. The implication of the question was obvious. After obtaining citizenship I would revert to Islam. My Christian profession was a mere sham and was not to be taken seriously.

Anyone who had heard the story of my conversion and knew of the persecution I had endured from my own family would never have thought of asking me such a question. Did Jesus not add to his saying that those who have left everything would receive a hundredfold with persecutions? I had received a hundredfold. Must I not be willing and ready to face persecution also? Thus I was able to answer my questioner calmly and simply: 'I will return to Pakistan one day if it is the Lord's will. I was happy there and I love my adopted family. Jesus knows this.'

While I was in Bedford I received a phone call from Prahbu Guptara, presenter of the television programme *Come Close*. He wanted me to appear in one of his productions on Central Television. It would be screened in Birmingham. The programme would last for fifteen minutes, not a very long time, but precious time when devoted to the proclamation of Jesus' message. This for me was another miracle. I prayed earnestly the night before:

Lord, let this be for your glory. You said that you would give me the right words whenever I needed them. I need them now. Take my mind and let it think your thoughts, and my lips that they may speak your words. Grant that many hearts may be moved by your Spirit to respond to my testimony and receive you as their Lord and Saviour.

I believed my Lord would hear and answer my prayer.

It had been agreed that Susan, her father, and her brother and our Asian pastor would accompany me, and that Thelma Marks would be my interpreter. It was a bright and beautiful morning when we all gathered at the studio in Birmingham. It was like a dream to me, being in the studio with the television lights on me. Was this really happening to me I wondered. Then I remembered that a greater light had shone upon me and the evidence was there for all to see. As a matter of fact, this latter light was the one I was about to talk about. Fortunately, there were not many people there, only the producer, the director and two or three technicians. The presenter put the questions to me and with the help of Thelma I answered as well as I could.

At the end of the interview the director thanked me. I could not help noticing that he had been moved by my story and seemed even embarrassed that God should have raised up a former cripple to make others aware of the truth of the Christian Gospel. But I knew that I was nothing in myself and by myself. Through Jesus Christ, however, I could do all things.

When I was a Muslim I could do nothing for Islam. I was a cripple, useless. But Jesus Christ had healed me and had given me new life, new hope, new purpose, and new meaning for my life. Nothing could stop me from declaring His message: 'I am the Way, the Truth, and the Life.' Now I could point the Way to my fellow Muslims. My heavenly Father had indeed become my Father. Daily I was experiencing his love and I wanted them to share it too.

It was becoming obvious to all those concerned and connected with my ministry that Oxford would provide a better base from which to travel. It was more accessible to other places and there would be less travelling for me. Consequently, on 4th February, Susan accompanied me to Huddersfield to collect my few belongings. We returned by coach on 8th February. Thus I took up residence with Susan's family in Oxford. Susan now accompanied me on all my trips.

Our first trip together was to Coventry. I had not been there before. A Pakistani Christian family came to fetch us. In the evening we had a gathering of about twelve to fifteen English people. Susan translated for me. Among our guests was a Sikh who seemed very impressed with my testimony. After the meeting he said to me. 'Sister Gulshan, I have not heard such a testimony before although I have met many Christians, Pakistani, Indian, and English. I work in a bank and I meet a lot of them and yet I have never heard any Christian say that Jesus has touched them. Can you come to my home tomorrow and talk to my wife and me about Jesus Christ? There is so much we would like to know. I realize that you are on a short visit, but we would be grateful if you could come.'

This personal invitation gave me great joy. 'Come and tell about Jesus' he had said! What greater privilege could I have? I accepted gladly. When Susan and I arrived the next day, his wife had prepared an excellent lunch for us. The table was laden with every kind of dish we could have hoped for. They even had gifts for us. I did not like to receive gifts in this way. The only and the greatest gift I had to offer was the gift of salvation in Christ Jesus our Lord and that was free. My testimony to it was free also. I hesitated to accept their gift, but when it seemed that I would offend them I had to take it.

After lunch we sat down to what I expected to be a discussion about Jesus and his death on the cross for our sins but unfortunately, the family were more interested in prayer for their various needs. And these had nothing to do with salvation. Their problems centred around their two sons. With the elder one they had little or no relationship and this distressed them. Their younger one was sitting an examination and they were anxious about that.

I was disappointed. I wanted them to see Jesus, the Son of God, as their Saviour and to seek his will for their lives, but all they seemed to want was for Jesus to take their difficulties away. Yet I remembered that I was the same once. In my crippled state all I wanted was to be healed physically: in contrast, Jesus wanted to give me new life and new hope.

I gently said to them, 'Start praying for yourselves. Ask Jesus to lead you in the right path, for he wants us first to seek his kingdom and his righteousness and then he will give us whatever else we need.'

I reflected sadly that it is so easy for us to allow our physical and human needs to veil our more urgent and spiritual needs from our eyes. Jesus would tear this veil away if we allowed him to, but so often we prefer to cling to it. Susan and I returned to Oxford to find an invitation to go to Scotland waiting for us. We were to join a Christian brother in East Ham, London, and from there to go by train to Glasgow.

In Glasgow I addressed several groups but it was one house meeting which stands out in my memory. One of the couples present was having marital problems because the wife was supposed to be demon-possessed, and I was asked to pray for her. The family gave me details of her problems. They said that at certain times she would become so violent that she would accuse her husband of wanting to kill their children and then she would disown him. When she recovered from such outbursts she would be full of remorse. Her husband and father pleaded with me to help her. We had a prayer session for her which lasted for nearly eight hours and at the end of it she said, 'Thank God I feel well again.' A few months later when I saw her husband he was beaming and said that he and his wife were reconciled and that they were both well and happy.

From Glasgow we returned to London and stayed with the Din family until the end of the month. This family was later to play a major role in my ministry. Five days after we had returned to Oxford, we were invited to Southall where we were the guests of Mrs Daniell, a Pakistani Christian who was a widow. We joined her for worship in a Methodist church on Sunday and every evening from Monday to Saturday we had meetings in the church hall. Strangely, there seemed to be no fruit to our ministry.

Then, one day towards the end of the week, two Indian ladies, both non-Christians, came to Mrs Daniell's house in a very distressed state. They owned a big clothes shop in the High Street and were troubled by the mysterious appearance in their shop of meat and blood on the floor. Despite the tightest security, every day when they opened the shop they found these objects lying on the floor. Not only were they disgusted and afraid, but being superstitious women, they suspected some evil purpose behind it.

They needed help and came to ask for my prayer. They said that they were convinced that Jesus could deliver them from this evil. I was invited to their shop. I had a hard time persuading them that this was not part of my ministry. I did not wield any magical power. 'First open your hearts and ask Jesus to enter your lives and save you from your sins. It is salvation you need first, not this deliverance from some evil designs of people. I will not ask you to kneel and pray with me for I can see that you are not ready for that. Believe first and then I will pray for you.'

They took this graciously and went home. This was not what they had come for. However, they returned the next day. 'Sister Gulshan, we are ready to open our hearts to Jesus Christ. Please pray for us.' I could see that they had not come to this decision easily. Maybe this occasion was the climax of a long time of seeking. We prayed together and then I took some water and prayed over that. I told them to pray every day and then to sprinkle this water around the shop. Two days later they reported that their shop had been cleansed and they expressed much gratitude for their deliverance. When they came to tell me this, just before I was about to leave, they brought one of their expensive dresses for me. Once again I had to protest. I did not want to be treated like a Hindu priest and be given gifts for my services. I wanted them to be faithful to Jesus Christ and to remember Him when their business became successful. But they insisted. 'Please accept this gift as an expression of our love for God and for you.'

Thus, this curious episode ended with two new converts and what had seemed like a barren ministry suddenly became fruitful. What fruit they themselves would bear for Jesus in their daily contact with Hindus and Pakistanis we would probably never know: but Jesus will know and to his name be the glory. Susan's father came to fetch us and we returned to Oxford, satisfied that we had accomplished something for our Lord.

There was hardly any time to relax, however, for a few days later we were on our way back to East Ham where we again stayed with the Din family. I had been invited to give my testimony at St. Helen's church. I knew that the service was going to be recorded but I had not the slightest idea what far-reaching consequences it would have nor that it would mark the beginning of the end of my frequent travels around the country.

In the congregation was Noble Din, the son of our hosts. He was a Pakistani Christian who worked in Saudi Arabia and came to England to visit his parents whenever he was on holiday. It was he who had arranged for me to speak at the Sunday evening service. Noble was so impressed by my testimony of what Jesus had done for me that he thought that it ought to be published in a book. I can only say that I believe that God's Holy Spirit was at work that night. This new opportunity to witness to Jesus exceeded my wildest hopes.

Noble was in a good position to influence this, since he had a friend who was at that time the managing director of the publishers, Marshall, Morgan and Scott. He persuaded his friend, John, to listen to the tape recording. John became very interested and lost no time. Within a few days it had been agreed that my testimony would be published by his company. I was asked to promise not to sign a contract with any other publishing company. Thelma Sangster was invited to work with me to write the story in attractive English, and Noble Din would act as my interpreter.

It might seem that that prophecy made at my birth was about to be strangely fulfilled. Yet it was quite the opposite to that which had been predicted, for it was not fame for myself in which I was interested. On that glorious January morning after I had been healed, the story of it had spread like wild fire throughout the community. Friends and relatives from near and far flocked to witness the amazing sight – Gulshan Fatima Shah, the cripple for nineteen years, was walking!

But now, with the publication of my miraculous healing in a book, the good news of what Jesus had done for me would spread even further and bring even greater glory to his name. More important, his message 'I am Jesus. I am Immanuel. I am the Way, the Truth, and the Life. I am alive, and I am coming soon' would resound through its pages. This for me was another miracle.

Chapter 10

The Asian Convention

It was crowded in Oxford in May. Tourists of every description and speaking many languages were beginning to pour into the city. The guides were kept fully occupied shepherding their little flocks of visitors around the many colleges, pointing out this and that piece of interesting architecture and telling tales connected with the various monuments. One of the most inspiring must have been the crosses in the Broad, marking the spot where Hugh Latimer and Nicholas Ridley were burned at the stake for their faith on 16th October 1555. Repeated down the centuries must have been the famous words of Hugh Latimer: 'Be of good comfort, Master Ridley, and play the man. We shall this day light such a candle by God's grace in England as I trust shall never be put out!'

Asian Christians were holding their annual convention in Oxford on 14th May 1983 and I was invited to be the main speaker. This was such a privilege that I spent a lot of time in prayer and meditation for it. All seemed to be going well and yet there was a dark cloud hanging over my life which was soon to reveal itself.

The convention was due to start at 10.00 a.m. Around 9.00 a.m. my friends from Huddersfield arrived. 'We have a letter for you Sister Gulshan. As we did not have your full address and we knew we would be seeing you soon, we kept it so that we could give it to you personally.' They handed me the letter and I opened it immediately.

Its contents deeply shocked me. My second adopted daughter, Razia, had died almost a month ago and had been buried. She had had cancer and I had no idea of it. The shock must have been obvious on my face and my friends became concerned. They made me sit down and offered me a glass of water. I shared the tragic news with them. They became very distressed. 'If only we had known what was in that letter we would made a greater effort to send it on. The least we could have done today would have been to keep it until after your address. Please forgive us; we had no idea.'

Despite my grief I could not find it in my heart to chide them. 'You could not have known what news you were bringing me. Please, don't upset yourselves.' I was trying hard to regain some composure, and asked to be left alone for a few minutes. There was only one thing to do: I took the letter to Jesus: 'O Jesus, you know how I feel at this time. My heart is full of grief. How can I address this large crowd this morning with such a heavy heart? Help me to bear this suffering so that I can deliver my testimony to the glory of your name. Only you can give me the strength I need. Thank you for hearing my prayer.'

My Lord answered me with the most wonderful promise. 'One day you will see Razia.' This hope, coming from my Lord Himself, pierced the gloom which had settled upon my mind, and my heart rejoiced in his goodness to me. How this hope transforms even the most tragic situation! No longer need we part from our loved ones with bitterness of finality, of never being able to see their faces again. St. Paul's words came ringing in my ears:

For if the dead are not raised, then Christ has not been raised, your faith is futile and you are still in your sins. Then those also who have fallen asleep in Christ have perished. If for this life only we have hoped in Christ, we are of all men to be most pitied. (I Corinthians 15:16–19).

I knew then without a shadow of doubt what the emphasis of my message for that morning must be. By the time the service reached the point when I was to speak, I felt as if the hope of eternal life which had penetrated all my thoughts and feelings was like a bulb within me shining out in the darkness. I was able to give my testimony with power and conviction. Many hearts were touched and as I left the pulpit many of the audience hugged and kissed me. At the end of the service people were streaming to the front to dedicate their lives anew to Jesus Christ or to offer him their lives for the first time. It was thrilling to watch. In his hands even tragedy could be used to honour his name and lift us to look beyond it to the glorious life he has promised us. I knew that Razia had already entered that life.

When Susan and I returned home, we found the house full of people waiting to see me. They were eager for me to visit their own churches and share my message with them. So many doors were being opened for me that I felt that I would have to be two or more people to enter them all. Reluctantly, I had to refuse some of these invitations for I already had many commitments. On Sunday afternoons I went regularly to the 3.00 p.m. service in the Asian church in Oxford. On Tuesdays I led the Bible study and on Wednesdays the prayer meeting. However, I promised to visit some of the churches to which I had been invited whenever I could. I was glad when the day ended.

That night when I got into bed around 9.00 p.m. memories of Razia came flooding into my mind. She had been a Christian, a Roman Catholic. I recalled how she came to be my adopted daughter. Her mother lived in a village far away in the country and I had gone there to give my testimony. Her mother was very ill and after I had prayed for her she said to me, 'Sister Gulshan, I have not long to live. When I die will you look after my children for me?' I promised her that I would and six months later when she died I brought her children to Faisalabad and legally adopted them. There were four of them: Edwin, Zenith, Razia, and Sheila. After Edwin completed his education I sent him to be an apprentice welder. Zenith worked as a nurse and had helped her mother to keep the other children together. Their father had died when Edwin was only six months old.

Razia's wedding had been a wonderfully happy occasion for me. The week-long celebrations for her wedding were the happiest experiences I had had for a long time and helped me to relive the joyful wedding festivals of my own brothers' and sisters' weddings. Razia's wedding had not been half as grand, but her marriage had been a good one; sadly, as I now learnt, it was not meant to be a long one. She had died just one year later.

My last contact with Razia had been at the station in Faisalabad in 1982 when I was leaving for England. I remembered how, with a beaming face she had looked up to me and said, 'Here Ma-ji. I made it specially for you.' It was an embroidered handkerchief and in it was a picture of Jesus. I got out of bed and found it, tears streaming down my face. If only I had gone back to Pakistan in January 1983 as I had intended to, I would have seen her alive. My natural feelings began to surface. I knew where she was now, but the pain of human death and parting filled me. I shall never see her face again in this life. The chain had been broken and the missing link left a gap which hurt. I did not think Jesus would be displeased with me. Did he not weep at the grave of his friend Lazarus? In time my broken heart would be mended. As I lay there, the pain of death and the hope of eternal life struggled for ascendancy in my being and eventually I fell asleep exhausted.

In the following weeks I immersed myself in my travelling ministry. On 19th May Susan and I went to Didcot where I met and had fellowship with an Asian family. To some of the other meetings, a whole group of us would go, taking our musical instruments with us. Whenever one of the men played the tabla and the dolki I often felt as if I were at a wedding. I was beginning to understand why Jesus described life in heaven as being at a banquet.

Marriage gives so much pleasure in life but it can also bring problems and divide even the closest of families. Occasionally I would find myself drawn into these situations as people sought my advice. For converted Asians the problems of marriage are compounded and exacerbated. Muslim in-laws always insist that daughters-in-law become Muslim after their marriage to Muslim husbands. Several young women have asked for my help in deciding whether to marry Muslim men. Often they are told that people of other faiths are 'just as good' and therefore intermarriage would present no problems. My advice, however, has always been the same: seek Christ first then a husband. If you marry a Muslim man you will not be able to practise your Christianity. You will not be allowed to go to church or have fellowship with other Christians. A Muslim man is allowed to have four wives and you will not be able to stop him taking another woman if he wants to. In such ways, I have sought to open the eyes of those who have come to me for help.

I did not have many occasions to meet with non-Christian people but one such occasion was provided for me in Birmingham when I was invited by some Asian elders. I found myself addressing many Sikhs and Hindus. Many of them asked for healing and the Lord wonderfully confirmed his message with immediate results. This surprised those who were not used to seeing the results of prayer. Unfortunately, many came to see Jesus Christ only as a healer of the body's illnesses and not as the Son of God who had died for their sins. On this occasion the healing acted as a barrier to their conversion. This is one of the reasons why I do not like to over-emphasize healing. Ordinary medical help can cure bodies but only Jesus Christ can cure the soul and bring salvation. Did he not say: 'What does it profit a man to gain the whole world and lose his soul?'

In response to some of the invitations extended to me after the Oxford convention, I went to Leicester. After I gave my testimony, many came to believe in the Lord Jesus Christ and were convinced that the light of the Gospel was truly shining in the darkness in their midst. Jesus was alive and was bringing in his sheep. Those who heard me longed to join with me in bringing other sheep and invited me to return so that they could bring their non-Christian friends to hear my message.

Another visit was to Southampton, when Fazad and

his wife came to fetch Susan and me. Fazad works in a computer factory and has two children. One of their friends, Zenib, who had been under their influence for a long time, committed herself to Jesus Christ after she heard my testimony. Fazad and his wife were overjoyed, but Zenib's Muslim friends were not. They kept on asking her about her new faith and denouncing her for abandoning Islam. She became so harassed over this that she sent an urgent request to me: 'Please, Sister Gulshan, could you come and answer their questions? I am fed up with trying.' I said I would go but not immediately.

It was at this time that I received an invitation that could have changed the pattern of my ministry if I had accepted it. Some Christians in Bristol who had no pastor invited me to become their pastor. They promised to do anything I wanted. They would give me all their offerings if I consented. For me, however, this was another temptation to depart from the path I had been asked to walk on. I had to say: 'I am very sorry, I cannot accept your invitation even though I am honoured to be asked. To be a pastor is not my calling. I have been called to be an evangelist and that is what I must be.'

They were a determined group of people. 'Could you come every Sunday and take our service then?' In response, I did go with Susan's brother for a few Sundays. Sometimes they almost pleaded with me: 'Please become our pastor and stay in Bristol.' The Asian girls who were married to Muslim men said to me: 'We have no one here who can speak our language and feed us from the Bible. Please reconsider your decision.' Eventually I managed to get them to accept my position.

Through a converted Hindu who worked as an

evangelist in Oxford I was able to have a delightful experience in the city's most prestigious hotel, the Randolph. Built in 1864, it stands in the heart of the city and is famed for its beautiful architecture and elegance. Never in all my life did I imagine that one day I would have the honour of entering it as a guest speaker. The Lord does do marvellous things through his servants. My only other experience of an English hotel was when my father brought me to London to find a cure for my crippled condition. Here at the Randolph I was to be an honoured guest. What a startling contrast to the usual church or school hall!

The Businessmen's Christian Fellowship was holding one of its meetings in the Spires Restaurant in the Randolph on 20th June. I was invited to be one of the speakers and our friend the evangelist obtained three tickets, one for me, one for himself and one for Susan's brother who was to be my interpreter. When I entered the room the music was so beautiful, the lights so splendid and the furnishings the best I had ever seen that I began to feel like a princess. God my Father was indeed the King of kings and I, his daughter, was being given the privilege and freedom to enjoy his many gifts.

The whole atmosphere was dream-like to me. Businessmen do not normally mingle with ordinary people and yet here I was addressing them. It seemed incredible. The two or three other speakers who had been invited never had a chance to speak. As these well dressed and elegant looking gentlemen listened at the way Jesus had healed me and guided me to come to England, they became enthralled and encouraged me to go on. 'We can listen to the others anytime but we are not likely to hear you again,' they said to me.

After the meeting they all shook my hand and said

how moved they were by my testimony. My account
of the persecutions I suffered as a result of my faith
made them realize anew how precious Christianity is.
It was also a new experience for them to hear a
Muslim girl speaking so freely. The President of the
meeting put his hand on my shoulder and said to me,
'The Lord has been speaking to me tonight. We
should all be witnesses for Christ. Thank you for
reminding us of this.'

We had a real feast that night. There were so many
dishes that I did not know which one to choose! What
I chose was excellent and so also was the fellowship.

Afterwards, I realized that it was time to honour
my promise to Zenib to make a second visit to Southampton. Aman Jeet and his wife Krishna accompanied
Susan and me, on 18th June to the port from which
great ocean liners had sailed to India and other parts
of the world.

Here I encountered the biggest challenge to
explain my faith to a Muslim family. This was no
ordinary family but one that was almost fanatical in
their belief and practice of Islam. They could not
accept that I, a member of a Sayed family and daughter of a Pir, could possibly have become a Christian.
If that were true then I was an infidel, an unbeliever
and a traitor. They nevertheless invited me into their
home.

The mother was the most vociferous. Her first question to me was: 'Have you left Islam?'

'No,' I replied, 'I have not left Islam. I have true
Islam.'

This seemed to amaze her and she reacted immediately with: 'But in your preaching you are saying that
Jesus Christ is the Son of God. If you had true Islam,
as you say you have, you would know that the Holy

Quran teaches that Jesus was a prophet just like Abraham, Moses, and the others. How can you say you have true Islam and say this at the same time? You contradict yourself. Muslims do not claim that Muhammad (may peace and blessings of Allah be upon him) was a son of God. He was a man, God's prophet, his last and final one. You ought to know that.'

She was talking to me as if I were ignorant of Islam. My pride was hurt and I was tempted to relate to her how my father had meticulously taught me what I ought to believe but I restrained myself and answered her calmly, recalling Jesus' words to the apostles: 'Do not be anxious beforehand what you are to say, but say whatever is given to you in that hour for it is not you who speak but the Holy Spirit.' And I continued: 'Jesus was more than a prophet. He did not only proclaim God's message to the people but he was God in human form. He told me on the night he healed me that he was Immanuel. Immanuel means God with us. I cannot say that he was simply a prophet.'

'So you are saying that Jesus is greater than our prophet?'

'That God used Muhammad to turn the Arabs from the worship of idols to worship of the one living God, I do not deny but Jesus was more than that. As the Son of God he forgives us our sins.'

'And what do you mean by that? Our Quran teaches us that only Allah forgives sins and we must pray continually to him to ask for forgiveness of our sins. I don't suppose you know that, do you?' she asked in growing disbelief that I should be so lacking in understanding.

Quietly, I replied, 'I know that we are told to pray

for our sins to be forgiven. But what I am telling you is this. That God our Father has forgiven us our sins in Jesus Christ. All we have to do is to accept his gracious forgiveness.'

'Without praying for it, without seeking Allah's mercy?' she asked.

'We must pray for willing hearts and spirits to accept what God is freely offering to us. Jesus died on the cross for our sins.'

'All this talk about a cross baffles me. How can a man dying on a cross bring forgiveness to anyone. Your brain has obviously been affected.'

'Jesus was not just a man dying on a cross. He was the Son of God who paid the penalty for our sins so that we might be forgiven and set free to love God. The wages of sin is death. His dying meant that the wages for our sin have been paid.'

'This is too complicated for me. How can I understand such teaching? The Quran is so much simpler.'

I then read St. Paul's words to the Corinthians to her:

> For the word of the cross is folly to those who are perishing, but to us who are being saved it is the power of God . . . We preach Christ crucified, a stumbling block to Jews and folly to Gentiles . . . [1 Corinthians 1:18, 23].

'I am not perishing,' she retorted; 'my family, they are not perishing either. Who is perishing? As far as I can see it is you who are perishing – by giving up Islam.'

'All those are perishing who do not accept that God in Jesus Christ has forgiven us our sins and has opened the door to eternal life through him to all. People who do not want to have their sins forgiven or do not want to spend eternity in God's presence are perishing. Through Jesus, we have eternal life which begins here and now. I have that new life in me.'

'How can a man who has died on a cross give eternal life to anyone?' she asked. 'Our holy Quran tells us that when we die we will go to Paradise and have all the blessings we seek. That is when our new life begins, not now. You are sillier than I thought.'

She was almost echoing the words of my brother-in-law, Blund Shah: 'It says even in your Bible that only a man who is cursed will die on a cross and how can a man who is cursed give life to others?'

I had tried to explain that the 'curse' was our sins, but to no avail. So this time I tried another approach. 'You see, Jesus, the Son of God, did not remain on the cross. He rose from the dead. He is alive. I know. He appeared in my room and healed my crippled body. I am not asking you to worship a dead man but a living Saviour.'

'Oh yes, your healed body. I wish you had never been healed!'

I looked at her with pity even as I did my brothers who would have preferred to see me dead rather than hear me say that Jesus Christ was the Son of God and my Saviour. 'You may wish I were still a cripple but God, my Father, loves me and has put new life into my wasted limbs.'

'You keep calling God, "father". I suppose you pray to him now.'

I seized the opportunity to repeat the beautiful new prayer Jesus had given to me. I had hardly finished when she added: 'Am I to believe that you have discarded all our beautiful prayers for this one?'

'Yes,' I answered; 'I now pray to a God who is not

unknowable and far away, but one who is near and dear to me. His Word, the Holy Bible is my most precious treasure and this is what I read and study daily.'

'Are you expecting us to start reading that book as well? When we Muslims read the Quran together, its beautiful poetry lifts us on to another plane. We are united in one wave of love and devotion to Allah. What would your Bible do for us? It has been translated into so many different languages and even different versions of the same language that people cannot possibly have the same sense of oneness when they read it. You are asking us to exchange what is superior for something inferior.'

'I am not asking you to do anything you don't want to do. I can only put before you what Jesus has told me. You must make your own response and decide whether you prefer darkness to light.'

'You are very arrogant and presumptuous,' she said as she showed us to the door. 'I will have no more to do with you. You have betrayed our faith. An infidel is not welcome in my home.'

Chapter 11

To Canada

To my family in Pakistan the possibility of my leaving our secure home and family to go abroad by myself was unthinkable. But Jesus Christ had made the unthinkable a reality. He had guided and directed my step all the way and now, in August 1983, he was leading me beyond the shores of England to Canada, the second country my family had pointed out as a Christian one to which I could not conceivably go.

The tape recording of my testimony made by my friends in Pakistan had been sent to various countries, including Saudi Arabia, Iran, Iraq, Kuwait, and Morocco. It had also reached Canada. Asian Christians in Canada hold a yearly convention in Alberta to which guest speakers are invited. The pastor-in-charge was a Canadian but one of his elders was an Asian businessman who had heard my testimony and suggested that I should be the main speaker.

When I received the invitation, I prayed about going and decided that if it were Jesus' will, I would go. Shortly afterwards, I received two tickets, one for Susan and one for myself. I took this as a sign that it was the Lord's will that we should go. We felt elated with this new door Jesus was opening for me. Susan was particularly excited and threw herself with great enthusiasm into preparation for our first transatlantic flight.

On arrival in Alberta we were greeted with great love and affection by the Asian and the Caribbean

Christians. As in Pakistan, we were garlanded so many times that our necks became heavily weighed down. The scent of flowers filled the air. This was not the only touch of Pakistan that was in store for me. Who should I find in Alberta but the very pastor who had baptized me, the Reverend Aslam Khan?

The road to baptism had not been an easy one for me to take. It had meant cutting myself off completely from my family. Once I was convinced that it was the only step I could take to show the change which had taken place in my heart and my vowed intention to give my allegiance to Jesus Christ, there was no turning back. The Major in the Salvation Army who had given me my first Bible left me in no doubt of the danger I was incurring.

'Do you realize what may happen if you do this? You may never be able to return home again. Your family may even try to kill you. Oh yes, even as loving a family as yours can change completely when they see one of their number leaving the Muslim faith.'

This warning had come as no surprise to me. I remembered what my brother Safdar Shah had said to me: 'For the sake of Islam we can murder you. It says so in the Holy Quran.'

But I had made up my mind. I could not be an effective witness for Jesus Christ without making this open declaration of faith, so I said to him: 'Jesus Immanuel has told me that I must be his witness, and baptism is the next step for me. I must obey or I will forfeit this peace I now have. It is better for me to die with Christ than to live without him.' To this he had replied 'So be it then,' and arranged for me to go with his wife to a house on the Karachi Road, run by the Reverend and Mrs Aslam Khan who cared for converted Muslims. Meeting them again brought back vivid memories of those early days of my walk with Jesus.

In fact, after my baptism, they had both become Aba-ji (father) and Ama-ji (mother) to me. My relationship to Ama-ja did not get off to a good start, however. She expected me to help with the domestic chores and as I had had no previous experience of such work I was not very good at doing them, and this had displeased her. I remember how tempted I was to return home to my comfortable bed, the tender care of my aunt and uncle, the life of ease with servants to do everything.

I became very unhappy and in desperation one night I cried out to Jesus: 'I have surrendered myself to you and I feel I am on the right track yet I am treated like this. Why?'

He answered me in a still small voice: 'I am always with you. They cannot harm you.' His words brought peace to my heart and the spirit of rebellion and temptation left me. The example of Jesus when he washed and dried his disciples' feet rose up before my eyes and became from then on the perfect example of humility and service which I felt determined to emulate. My relation to Ama-ji improved after that.

With Aba-ji the problem was a different one. I remembered distinctly the conversation I had with him after I was baptized and emerged from the tank of water with new life bubbling within me and with my new name, Esther. The friends who had gathered for the ceremony left. 'How do you feel?' he had asked. 'Fine,' I said, 'but now I want to witness to what has happened to me?'

He would have none of this. 'You can witness by your actions. It is not necessary to witness by your mouth also.' Not easily put off I had said, 'But I believe that Jesus wants me to witness. Can I speak in the church?' He persuaded me not to make public statements. 'You have a witness in the home to fulfil. God will accept that.' It was he who later helped me to get a job as a housemother at the Sunrise School for the Blind.

Meeting them again in Alberta was filled with emotion. They had since learnt of my conversion experience and of the sufferings I had endured because of it. Isn't it strange that during those five weeks when I was with them in their house on the Karachi Road, and under their observation to see if I were a genuine convert, they had never asked me how I came to know Jesus? It is no wonder that when we embraced each other, they wept. People asked if I were their daughter!

In their presence at the Asian Christians' conference in Alberta, I preached the Gospel and gave my testimony. The message I was longing to give them was Jesus' own words: 'I am alive. I am coming soon.'

'He is coming,' I announced. 'Are you ready to receive him?' But this was too big a challenge to consider. They were not prepared for this. It was sufficient that Jesus had touched me with his healing power and raised me up. That confirmed their belief that he does work miracles today but to prepare ourselves for his coming – that was something else!

My message had a mixed response. Some wondered how I could believe all that Jesus told me only after one encounter. My immediate acceptance of Jesus seemed strange to them. In their experience in Pakistan, they had seen in open air meetings, people being invited night after night to accept Jesus as Saviour, without any reaction. One family even said to me; 'You are happy because Jesus has given you healing and salvation. If he gives us a similar experience we too will believe all you say.' I committed everything to the Lord.

We had one interesting contact with a Sikh family. Bima, their four-year-old daughter was a diabetic and also suffered from asthma. She often had difficulty breathing. On meeting me she turned to her mother and said; 'Mother, after Sister Gulshan prays for me I will be able to eat everything. You will not have to choose what I eat and what I don't eat anymore.' Such confidence in Jesus from a four year old was very moving. How true it is that from the lips of children God has ordained praise (Matthew 21:16).

The family invited me to their home and to their immense joy after I prayed for Bima, she was completely healed. The personal contacts renewed us in mind and spirit. I met a widow whose husband, a medical doctor, had committed suicide. In his hand she had found a letter expressing his desire to be buried like a Christian. The widow had had no idea that her husband had accepted the Christian faith but she desperately wanted to fulfil his last wishes. She had found his family strongly opposed to this idea since Sikhs practise cremation only. Eventually she was able to persuade them to honour his last wishes. This I believe was the first step she herself had taken on the road to accepting Jesus Christ for after she heard my testimony, she committed herself to the Lord Jesus Christ as her Saviour.

Encouraged by these two incidents, we were able to enjoy some time in the beautiful Jasper Mountains in Alberta.

From there Susan and I flew to Toronto. We were taken to see the spectacular Niagara Falls. What awe and wonder filled me as I beheld this magnificent sight! Susan, again displaying her enthusiasm which nearly always outstrips her courage, wanted to go into one of the river boats which cruised along the bottom of the Falls. I managed to discourage her.

I looked wistfully across the border to the United States. It was beyond me at the moment because I did not have a visa which would allow me to enter it. A Christian family in Dallas had invited me to go there but I had to decline the offer since my passport had been with the Home Office at that time. Nevertheless, I thought, smiling to myself, I have seen it. That would do for the moment.

My ministry in Toronto was to prove more fruitful. The Christians there had made pamphlets advertising the meetings at which I was invited to speak.

They gave me a warm welcome. The feeling of those who came to hear me was summed up in the words of one of them: 'Sister Gulshan, I have only heard your tape and read your leaflet but today I see you in front of me and I can see that everything is right. You are living proof that Jesus Christ is alive and his teachings are true.' This pleased me because it showed that all I was and what I was doing pointed only to Jesus Christ, and exalted him and not me.

It seemed that I could not go anywhere without encountering some marital problem on which I was asked to give my advice. This is such a delicate subject that I have always been hesitant to say too much, but the problems related to marriage of converted Muslims to Muslim men inevitably involve families on both sides; further, deep rooted traditions and customs are inextricably bound up.

One Christian man whose son had married a Hindu woman was very concerned over his daughter's proposed marriage to a Muslim man. He knew that promises made beforehand were not always kept. His son had been forced to worship at a Hindu temple although before the marriage his future wife had promised that he could go to church. And, as a grandfather, he had not been able to see his grandchildren. Now he did not want the same thing to happen to his daughter. He confessed his failure to bring them up strictly as Christians and now felt helpless. He implored me to speak to his daughter to get her to see the dangers ahead. His own faith seemed to be on trial so I agreed to speak to Rena.

Rena explained her situation to me. 'I am very much in love with Nazim and we want to get married. He is a student and not a resident of Canada. I have his promise that after our marriage I could still be a Christian and our children would be brought up as Christians. My father has nothing really to worry about.'

I felt much sympathy for her. For one so young to be caught up in this dilemma was a painful experience. I felt, however, that she should consider carefully this very important step, and pointed out several possibilities to her – that her Muslim in-laws might not accept her as a member of their family unless she lived like a Muslim; that her children would belong to no faith; that although she might remain a Christian she would not be able to practise her faith or try to tell others of it. It would have to be a secret faith. The greatest hurdle would be of course the possibility that he might want to marry more than one woman. Lastly, I put to her the unpleasant possibility: 'Could it be that your friend may be using you to gain permanent entry into Canada? You are a young Christian. Why rush into marriage? Ask Jesus to help you make the right decision.'

While I was talking, Rena sat at my feet and looked into my face. She did not try to argue with me. She quietly said: 'I promise to think about all you have said.' I offered to pray for her. Later I learnt that she had decided to end her relationship with her Muslim boyfriend. Her father was overjoyed. 'Thank God she now understands what peril awaited her if she had followed the course she was so set on following!' he exclaimed when he met me.

I had one other wonderful opportunity of witnessing to Jesus Christ in Toronto. Grace's father worked at a radio station in Toronto and he was able to arrange for me to give an interview. Thus my message reached hundreds more who could not hear me personally. The scope of my ministry had certainly widened since those early days in Pakistan when I thought that just travelling from one end of the country to the other was extensive! Now radio, television, and a book were to extend my ministry beyond my wildest dreams.

One insignificant incident served to bring back memories of those early days. Susan and I were not very good at carrying heavy cases so we travelled 'light'. I spilled some gravy on my shalwar kameeze one day and, because I needed it later in the day, I had to put on my pyjamas while Susan washed it. As she was doing this little chore for me, she turned to our hostess Grace and said, 'This is part of my own ministry.' Grace laughed and said, 'I used to do that as well when I lived with my sister Rachel in Rawalpindi and Gulshan stayed with us. She lived with us for three years.

Grace's family were converted Sikhs. Her brother-in-law is a pastor of a Brethren church. The mention of my stay with them took my mind back to my sister, Anis Bibi. I remembered so very clearly the morning my nephew, Khalid, arrived and said to me: 'Aunty, your sister is calling for you.' I sensed immediately that something was seriously wrong. I told Rachel and Grace that I had to go and see Anis Bibi and went straight away with my nephew.

When we arrived I made my way to my sister's room and found to my horror that she was dying. She opened her eyes and looked at me. 'Pray for me Gulshan. See, Jesus is here, and he is saying, "Come with me. Your time has arrived." ' I protested: 'No, you are my sister and my friend. You cannot go. If you go I shall be alone. Please do not leave me.'

My thoughts were focused upon myself and the knowledge that if she died my one and only friend in the family would be gone. This was unbearable. But again Anis Bibi said. 'See, Jesus is in front of me. I am happy to go with him. I would rather die now than live longer and depart from him.' This was a curious thing to say and I didn't understand it at the time. Then she made her dying request: 'Please Gulshan, will you give me a bath after I am dead?' Instead of answering, I placed my hands on her head and prayed. 'Lord Jesus Christ, Anis Bibi is your daughter. Have mercy on her. I know that when she dies she will be with you. Your will be done.'

When I opened my eyes she had gone. I was heart-broken. She was still so very young and seemed healthy. I could not endure this parting. I knew with my mind that Jesus' will was best and that one day I would see her again, but my heart had not been prepared for such grief.

It was 10.00 a.m. when Anis Bibi died. At 4.00 p.m. I gave her the bath she had asked for. This was the ritual washing of the front of the body, part of the funeral rites. My sister was buried in the evening. I tried to comfort my brother-in-law and his two daughters with the hope of resurrection but he and all his relatives were Muslim, and this hope did not mean anything to them. The girls begged me to stay but this was difficult with so many hostile relatives around. I returned with a grieving heart to Rawalpindi.

That night I spoke to Jesus: 'Lord, you didn't think about me when you took my sister. I know you love me and you loved my sister. But why was her life so short? It was you who brought her back to life when she died five years ago. Why bring her back only to take her away again so soon? What sort of love is your love if you allow me to go through such pain? Are you going to make me suffer all my life? I won't talk to you anymore!'

Such was the depth of my grief that I dared to speak to my Lord like this! Such boldness deserved the wrath of God. But our God is a God of love. How deep that love was I was soon to learn.

For one whole week I said no more prayers, as if I were punishing Jesus for taking my sister from me. I did read my Bible but I had no food and only drank water or tea. The family were concerned and alarmed. 'Please Gulshan, you must eat. You will get sick. You cannot cannot continue like this.' Even the children implored me to return to my normal self. The pain in my heart was too great, however. Food did not interest me.

I had taken to sleeping on a mattress on the floor of the room in which Elizabeth's husband normally held the services. (They had no church building at this time.) I used to sleep with the girls but after Anis Bibi's death I slept in here so as not to disturb them. The floor was carpeted and I was comfortable. Being alone made it easier for me to bear my grief and to read my Bible.

At the end of the week I was awake as usual at three o'clock in the morning. My thoughts turned to my nieces and I wondered what life would be like for them with a stepmother since my brother-in-law was certain to remarry. I sat up on my mattress. The wall was in front of me. The door was ajar and the moonlight was creeping in. Suddenly there was a very bright light in my room. I was surprised and wanted to examine it carefully. Then I saw Jesus's face and my sister's. She was smiling. No one said anything for awhile.

The silence was broken by Jesus' voice: 'Do you see why I took her? She is happy with me. Do you want to know why I took her? Look!'

With that he turned my sister round and to my horror I saw her back covered with red lines, like fire burns. Jesus said to me: 'This is what her husband did to her daily when she was praying.' Then I recalled her dying wish: 'Please Gulshan, give me my bath after I am dead.' Now I understood. She did not want anyone else to see how cruel her husband had been to her and how much he hated· her for her Christian profession and her prayers to Jesus. She wanted to protect his reputation even after she was dead. Such was her loyalty.

Jesus addressed me a second time: 'Your sister is happy. Why are you unhappy and cross with me? I couldn't bear her pain any longer. Did you want her to suffer more than she has already done?'

I was speechless. What could I say? I caught a glimpse of Jesus' love and I was so overcome with awe and wonder. His love was so deep, so lovely, so kind. How could I ever have doubted it? In this vale of tears he is never far away. My sister's courage filled me with admiration for her. She had suffered alone. She had not shared her pain with anyone, not even me. In heaven her suffering had ended. Her pain was gone. The scars could not cause her any more suffering. She was happy. There was nothing else I wanted. My burden of grief rolled off my back and I was renewed in mind and spirit, praising my Lord, feeling truly chastened that I had allowed myself to question his love, which was beyond my understanding.

Susan and I returned to England from Canada on 23rd September.

Chapter 12

Darkening Clouds

The contract for my book was signed in September 1983 after my return from Canada. On 4th October I began to work on *The Torn Veil* with Thelma Sangster. Noble Din, with whose parents we were staying, acted as my interpreter. Every morning Noble would fetch Thelma from the station and take her back in the evening. For two whole weeks I went over and over again the details of my experiences. It was hard work, but also very rewarding and provided a pleasant interlude from my itinerant ministry. Over the following five months I met with Thelma from time to time to give additional information and to go over what she had written. As the story of my life unfolded before me I marvelled at the wonderful way God, my Father, had dealt with me. And the end of February 1984 the manuscript was completed and sent to the publishers. There was a sense of great relief and a feeling of satisfaction as we commended it to the Lord and asked him to glorify his name by and through it.

While the completion of my story in written form was like a climax to my ministry, it did not stop me from going round the country to bear witness to Jesus Christ personally. There were always those who, like the apostle Thomas, would say; 'Unless I see in his hands the print of his nails and place my finger in the mark of the nails, and place my hand in his side, I will not believe.' Eight days later, when Jesus stood before the disciples in a closed room, he invited

Thomas to do just that. 'Put your finger here and see my hands and put out your hand and place it in my side; do not be faithless, but believing.' Then Thomas answered, 'My Lord and my God!'

So I believed that my body, touched and healed by the hand of Jesus, was a living proof of his power to heal and a sign that his message from God was true. Those who, in the first century, saw the works which Jesus did were led to believe that he was the Son of the living God. I hoped that seeing my restored body would lead others to make the same confession. Hence I responded to as many invitations as I could.

Susan and I were invited by an English family to Leicester. Mr Wilson showed us around Leicester which Susan especially enjoyed since she had a chance to do some shopping. She was pleased to be able to buy some jewellery for our pastor's wife. It was interesting to see so many Indian shops in Leicester.

Mr Wilson had arranged for me to address a gathering of Christian and non-Christian people. Among them were a mother and two daughters. The mother was English and her husband was a Muslim. After the meeting they invited me to their home to meet their father who was ill and in bed. He was one of those who believed that Christianity was for Europeans only.

As I was being introduced to the father he said to me outright: 'Before you say anything, let me say one thing. I don't want you to open your Bible. I won't open the Quran either. Tell me what has happened to you in your life. I don't want to listen to what is in the holy books. Close those books and open your life-book to me.' So I did. I described how I came to be a Christian, how Jesus had appeared to me and showed me the passages in the Quran about himself.

When I was finished, the father said to me: 'These are things I have been longing and waiting to hear. I am so pleased that you have come to my house and have told me your testimony. Only Jesus can come to homes and save people.' I then opened my Bible and spoke to him about Jesus Christ.

'Jesus loves you and this is why I am here. He is calling you to come to him today. Jesus will save you and give you eternal life. It's up to you to accept this and come to faith in Christ. When you give your heart to Jesus, He will come and heal you. Do you accept Jesus as your Saviour?'

'Yes' he answered. 'I believe because first Jesus came into your life in Pakistan and through him you have come to England and now you are in my home.'

'Jesus sent me,' I said. 'Without his permission I do nothing. It is his will that I am here today.'

After this exchange he confessed his sins and asked Jesus for forgiveness. The daughters and their mother rejoiced to hear this. Before I left I prayed for him.

Since I had arrived in England and begun my witnessing to Jesus, I had encountered very little open hostility, opposition or disagreement. Sadly, this was about to change. I believe that the devil was at work stirring up trouble for me. I suppose it would have been surprising if he had done nothing to stem the rising tide of witnessing to Jesus by addresses, by radio, by television, and soon by my book.

Throughout my ministry I have occasionally been called upon to settle disputes and give my opinion or advice about various issues. Marriage problems, as I have already explained, were the ones which more often than not cropped up. I never regarded myself as a pastor or marriage guidance counsellor and therefore was always very reluctant to be drawn into these. In a small, distinct, Asian community this was not always possible, however.

The occasion which became the focus for dissension was one of supposed infidelity which involved key people in our Asian congregation. Two married couples were having difficulty sorting out their relationships and the wife of one of them implored me to help. 'Please, Sister Gulshan, you love Jesus and his word is very precious to you. Show me what to do.' She explained her position to me.

I advised her to speak to her mother-in-law and to persuade her to discipline her son. She did so, but instead of her mother-in-law doing this, she took matters into her own hands and spoke to the other woman concerned, whose husband became irate and accused me of interfering in their domestic lives. I was most upset. From then on events got out of hand. I got more and more dragged in and every word I uttered seemed to be misunderstood. Inevitably, feelings began to run very high and divisions were created in the congregation.

Even trivial matters were taken and blown out of all proportion. Culture can sometimes present an apparently impenetrable veil to the light of the Christian Gospel. It is a lifelong quest to distinguish between those cultural aspects of life which are good and can become the vehicles of a richer Christian life, and those which would strangle at birth the new life of the Spirit. For example, one young couple had acquired the habit of using terms of endearment publicly and showing affection openly. This habit was offensive to both Asian parents and elders, who find it distasteful. When I rebuked this couple for causing offence unnecessarily, they were highly annoyed.

Divorce is another sensitive issue for Indians. It is often alleged that many Indian parents would rather see their daughters maltreated or even killed than to see them leave their husbands' home. It seems that in some cases the only honourable way to leave the marriage home is in a coffin! Consequently, living in a western culture where the divorce rate is very high, and trying to hold on to a different moral code creates many great tensions within families. For converts from Islam, Hinduism, or Sikhism this is even more difficult. Christianity is blamed for lowering standards of morality and that is one reason why there is sometimes such fierce opposition to conversion to Christ.

The whole atmosphere in Oxford among the Asian Christians was becoming unpleasant for me. However, events were taking place in Pakistan which would in the end remove me from all this. A letter arrived from Zenith, my other adopted daughter. 'Ma-ji,' the letter ran, 'Razia's husband would like to marry Sheila. Will you give your approval? His family are very anxious for this to happen.'

In Pakistan this is not an uncommon occurrence. Sheila was also a Christian and that is why his family were so interested in her. I was pleased with this request. I knew he was a good man and would make Sheila happy. Without hesitation, I replied, giving my consent and made arrangements for the engagement. The date of the wedding was set and I booked a return flight to Pakistan.

I felt that my witness for Jesus must continue despite the many difficulties which were casting a dark shadow over it. Susan and I went to Slough for a meeting in an Anglican church. The invitation came from the evangelist who had made it possible for me to attend the Businessmens' Christian Fellowship

Convention in Oxford. The congregation was mainly English but there were some Asians, mostly Pakistanis.

Some members of the congregation were very good at visiting and trying to make converts to the Christian faith. Through their ministry one Hindu family was converted, but the mother, a divorcee, was keeping her Christianity to herself. She found it difficult to confess to Christ openly. After the morning service we were invited to accompany two of the congregation to Dina's home. She had a high temperature and her leg seemed to be paralysed.

I asked her: 'Do you believe in Jesus Christ?' 'Yes', she replied. 'Then open your heart and give yourself to Jesus Christ today and he will heal you. Cast your burdens upon Christ and he will give you rest'. With such words I exhorted her.

As she spoke Urdu it was not difficult to communicate with her. She sat quietly for a while and then said to me: 'From the bottom of my heart I accept Jesus Christ as my Lord. I give my whole life into His hands. From now on I want to live my life in His presence.'

The two ladies who had taken us to Dina's house could not contain their joy. 'We have visited her several times but she has never made such a profession'. We all bowed our heads as I prayed for her.

When we were leaving her house the ladies asked me: 'Why did you not try to show her the falsity and weakness of her Hindu religion?' 'That is not my method.' I said. 'I try to present Jesus Christ as our Saviour and God our Father as our Creator and Redeemer. When she or anyone else recognizes these basic truths, the rest takes care of itself.' The next time I saw Dina was at the afternoon service, her fever gone and her leg no longer paralysed.

In early July, Susan and I made a visit to Huddersfield. Yacub's father was very pleased to see us and expressed his regret that I was leaving England later in the month. 'I am happy you came to England. Before you came the Muslims were so proud, claiming that Islam was such a superior religion. Now when they hear your testimony, they are more humble and find it hard to argue with us as much as they did. We shall miss you when you are gone.' My friends in Huddersfield have remained faithful to me throughout my time in England and this has been a constant source of joy and praise.

The dissensions in the Asian community in Oxford affected me in other ways. Susan was not allowed to accompany me to Pakistan. Her family dissuaded her. 'Sister Gulshan will only be gone a few months. There is no need for you to accompany her. In no time at all she will be back.' They succeeded. In the event, however, they were wrong. A few months turned into a year and even then the possibility of my returning seemed remote. But we parted with the hope of seeing each other again in the near future. Neither of us was aware of what was in store for me.

Knowing my financial position – I had no regular income – friends from near and far were very generous with their gifts. These began to arrive even from friends in Canada who heard of my proposed trip to Pakistan and the forthcoming wedding. I did not need to tell them how important a dowry was in Indian weddings. It seems that I had not calculated well when I decided to adopt three daughters! I have known families who had been impoverished for life by this custom of giving huge dowries to brides.

But this was an exciting time for me and I looked forward to the wedding and the joy of seeing family and friends again. It had been a longer visit than I had anticipated. I had been in England for nearly two years and during that time I had witnessed to Jesus Christ on every opportunity which had presented itself. Now, however, I could not help wondering: Had my work ended? My book would soon be published and the return ticket I had was to ensure that I would be back in time for its publication. Maybe that would be the real climax to the commission Jesus had given to me. I had no way of telling. I was not in charge of my life. I had put it in Jesus' hands. Deep down in my heart I faced the possibility that my ministry in the form it had taken up to this point was ending.

Chapter 13

Return to Pakistan

I looked forward to the day of my departure with mixed feelings. My family and friends in Pakistan had been clamouring for my return and I knew that our reunion would be full of happiness. But I had also made some very dear friends in England and I loved my ministry among them. There was much sadness in my heart as the day approached.

Laden with all the generous gifts I had been given, I left for the airport accompanied by Susan, her father and her brother. I was booked to fly to Faisalabad via Karachi and so had to spend one night in a hotel in Karachi. When I arrived the next day in Faisalabad, what a welcoming party awaited me! My sister Samina was there with her husband, their five daughters and three sons and of course, my own children, Sheila, Zenith and Edwin, and their grandfather.

Each one greeted me with a kiss and a garland of flowers. I was engulfed with a feeling of warmth and affection. I had almost forgotten what it was like to have so much love thrust upon me. My shiny blue shalwar kameeze and white coat were soon covered with garland upon garland of beautiful marigold flowers with an aroma that seemed to penetrate my senses.

Outside they had a car and a jeep waiting for me. We drove to my own six-bedroomed bungalow which my Christian friends had helped me to buy. As we arrived I was surprised but pleased to see all my

Muslim neighbours standing at their door to welcome me home. On greeting me they said how much they had missed me and thanked God for my safe return.

My sister and her family stayed with me for two days. There was so much to talk about. The children told me about their own little adventures and what each one was doing at school or at work. I was delighted to be 'in the know' once again and relished the little bits of information about the family, so insignificant in themselves, yet so full of the richness which makes family life interesting and unique.

We fixed Sheila's wedding date for September. After my sister and her family left, my daughters and I threw ourselves into the preparations for the wedding. Everyone loves a wedding. We bought furniture, crockery, cutlery and all the household goods that Sheila wanted. Susan would have enjoyed these shopping expeditions! My dowry was not as big as I would have liked, but Sheila knew and understood my financial position. She was happy that I was back among them and we could do all this together.

One week before the wedding I had to go to a meeting in Faisalabad. Our Muslim neighbours had a lodger, Ghulam Abdul. He came over just before we were about to leave. 'Please Gulshan, can I borrow your sitting room? I have visitors coming and there is no room for them where I am staying.' This may seem like an odd request, but in Pakistan this was not so unusual. Because of the way in which my bungalow was constructed, with an outer door opening out on to the street and with inner doors leading into the other rooms, it was possible for me to give him the key to the sitting room and lock all the others.

I took Zenith aside. 'Is he trustworthy? Should I let him have the key? What about you? Where will you stay?' I asked Zenith, not wanting to refuse the request and yet not very happy about granting it.

'Oh yes, he is alright. He is a good man. I will stay in the hostel at the hospital for the night.' So Zenith reassured me and I gave Ghulam the key. I thought he was a little excessive in his show of gratitude. With Sheila and Edwin I left for Faisalabad. We concluded our business and returned on the following day.

What a shock awaited me! As we tried to open the main door, we found that it was locked from the inside. Then Ghulam came out of one of the side doors. Without the slightest look of embarrassment on his face, he looked me straight in the eyes and said, 'This is my house, not yours.'

Horrified and shocked, I glared at him. This wasn't possible. He could not be doing this to me. Out of the goodness of my heart I had given him permission to use my sitting room to entertain his guests. Suddenly, I realized with dismay that these people were not his guests. He had brought his family and had occupied my very own house.

I appealed to my neighbours for help. I went first to the Roman Catholic family living not very far away. Surely they would know that this was my house and that my children have been living there for the past five years? I pleaded with them for help: 'Please, will you come and help me to get this man out of my house?' To my utter astonishment, they were completely indifferent to my cry. They did not want to get involved. They merely went back into their house and shut their door.

'We must go to the Police,' Sheila and Edwin kept repeating. I was reluctant to call the Police. I believed that I could make Ghulam see sense. No one just walks into the house of another and takes it over.

People just don't do that sort of thing. How wrong I was! Reasoning with him was to no avail. He insisted that it was his house. As a bus driver, Ghulam was allowed by law to possess a gun for his protection. When he threatened me with it I had no choice but to go to the police. Another shock was in store for me.

The Police officer who listened to my story was most unsympathetic. 'Next time you want to give your house key to someone,' he said, 'give it to me. I will take care of it for you.' Nevertheless, he had Ghulam brought to the station. As if he had some predetermined plan, Ghulam produced some legal documents which allegedly made him owner of the property. They were obviously false but I had no means of proving that.

The officer asked me: 'Have you anyone to support your claim to ownership?' I realized then that I had to convince him as well that the property was mine. I thought of the other neighbours; the ones who had greeted me so warmly when I arrived. 'Yes, my neighbours would,' I announced confidently.

Again, how mistaken I was! The hatred of the Muslims for me went deeper than I had imagined. They supported the intruder's claim. Their words of welcome on my return had only been superficial.

Was I having a nightmare, I asked myself. Was all this really happening to me? Must I face dispossession a second time? Had not the first by my own family been hard enough to bear? But it was no nightmare. It was real enough. For the second time I was homeless in this world. I reminded myself that the Son of Man himself had nowhere to lay his head during parts of his ministry.

This time my children would be homeless too. That

was a tragedy. The situation seemed hopeless. What could I do? The Police officer said to me: 'Who must I believe? Here, I have two sets of papers before me. One says you are the owner and another says that Ghulam is the owner.' Then I realized that I must find some other way of regaining my property. My younger brother was a lawyer but would he help me? I doubted it. If I returned to Islam, then yes, he would help me without any hesitation. That, however, was not an option for me.

With Edwin and Sheila I went to stay in a friend's house. But this incident had a greater effect upon me than I realized. Two days later, I suffered a stroke and remained unconscious for a whole week. When I regained consciousness I was in the University Church Hospital. Dr Samuel Nawab came to visit me with his family. He had his eight year old son with him. 'This is your boy,' he said to me smiling.

I looked at Abraham. My boy indeed! Even in my stricken state I had praise in my heart for God our Father who had answered my prayer so wonderfully. Abraham was the son Dr Nawab and his wife had longed for but thought they would never have.

I had been living with James, the hospital gardener, when I first met Dr Nawab. In a conversation with him, the doctor had mentioned that his wife was very ill with arthritis and there was no cure available for her. James knew that I had often prayed for people and they had been cured. He told Dr Nawab this. When James offered to introduce us, Dr Nawab was delighted, for he was a good Christian man and worshipped regularly with his family in the Methodist church.

Dr Nawab was one of two children. He had a sister who lived in a village outside Faisalabad. He had three daughters and would have liked a son to carry on his name. This was not to be, since his wife was afraid to go through another pregnancy. She was a school teacher and taught English.

Feeling sorry for the doctor, who had no brother and now no son, I prayed that they might have a son. This surprised his wife who was against the whole idea. 'It is dangerous and risky for me to have another baby. It would have been nice to have a son but not now,' she protested. I had no such fears or doubts. 'Mrs Nawab,' I said, 'I do not know when you will be healed or when you will have a son, but I have placed your situation before Jesus. When he answers, you will know.'

One year later she became pregnant and was very worried for herself and her baby, but I tried to reassure her. During her pregnancy her arthritis became better. Abraham was born in 1976. After the pregnancy Mrs Nawab suffered no more arthritis. From then on a very warm relationship grew up between us. The doctor would often say: 'I have two sisters now; one in the village, and you.' He came from a wealthy family and often shared his gifts equally between his sister and me. Whatever came from the village, whether it was rice, sugar, or sweetcorn, he would share with me.

To be regarded as his sister and for his son to be known as 'my boy' was an honour indeed. I had only been God's instrument in bringing this blessing to him but he showed his gratitude to God by his great kindness to me. While I was in hospital after the stroke he had me put in a private room and paid all the costs. He even instructed the nurses to make sure I exercised twice daily, and he personally supervised my treatment.

I had another interesting visit while I was in hospital. This time it was my elder brother Safdar Shah. He brought two Maulvi (teachers) with him. The purpose was clear to me. He loved me and was concerned about me, but he also loved his religion. He never gave up hope that one day I would return to Islam. Like some of the other members of my family, he saw my stricken state as a sign that Jesus had abandoned me. If ever they were going to win me back to our ancestral faith it was now. Hence the presence of the Maulvi.

My brother pleaded with me: 'Please give up Christianity and return to Islam. It is obvious that Jesus has forsaken you and we can't bear to see you in this condition. Please come back to us and we will give you everything you need and look after you.' Great affection welled up inside me as I thought of the depth of his love for me, but I was also very upset. He still had not understood what Jesus Christ meant to me. His invitation was a temptation which I had to resist no matter how helpless I was, and despite the fact that it was my own brother who was being used to tempt me.

'Dear brother,' I said, 'I know how much you love me and you are only doing this because you love me. But your concern for my body is misplaced. This body will not go to heaven. My soul is alive in Jesus Christ. I am safe in him. This illness is good for me. If I give up Christianity I will lose eternal life. This is more precious to me than anything else. Islam will not give me eternal life. Please go away and do not make me unhappy. Whatever my circumstances I will remain faithful to Jesus Christ.'

As was to be expected he became very angry. Underneath his anger, however, love for me still lingered. When he left, I found under my pillow 50,000 rupees. He knew I would refuse if he gave it to me so he just slipped it under my pillow and left. Medical treatment in Pakistan is very expensive and he knew that I had no independent source of income. How I longed for him to know Jesus as his Saviour. Then we could rejoice in our faith together and that special love which binds families to each other would blossom again. That was the last time I saw my brother alive.

After two weeks in hospital I returned to my friend's house in Faisalabad but had to make daily trips to the hospital for treatment. It was during this difficult time that Sheila's wedding took place. Poor Sheila! Left as an orphan and now almost without a dowry! We had lost the furniture we had bought together with all the furnishings, the crockery and the gifts I had bought from England. Ghulam had seen to that. I was forced to sell what I had. Nina, my friend in Kidlington, had given me a diamond and ruby ring as a present by which to remember her. I sold it so that I could pay for the wedding.

Our domestic situation now changed. With Sheila married and living with her husband, Zenith decided to live in the nurses' quarters. I thought that Edwin should return to the city and complete his apprenticeship. Before he left he went to the street where our house was so that he could say goodbye to one of his friends. Ghulam saw him and reported to the police that Edwin had threatened him with the result that Edwin was put in prison. I was distraught. I had to get him out. I had one remaining present. My Christian friends in Canada had given me an expensive watch. I sold it in order to pay for Edwin's release. Soon after he left the city. I was now left alone. What should I do?

It was my nephew, Khalid, who came to my rescue and became my helper and protector. He and I had always got along very well. No one else but he could have persuaded me to take the daring step of riding on his motor cycle. Khalid cared for me as if I were his own mother. There was nothing he would not do for me. For someone who was completely unaccustomed to domestic chores it was remarkable how he cheerfully did them for me. He never thought that as a Muslim he should not be doing this for a woman or that he was doing a woman's job.

Everyday he would get fresh eggs for me. He even tried to make chappatis with black chick pea flour which was supposed to be good for me. He would come home at lunch time to prepare lunch for me and every evening he would prepare an evening meal for the two of us. When he got home in the evening he would come up to me, anxiety written all over his face. 'Aunty, have you eaten your lunch? How are you feeling? Have you any pain?' Such was his deep concern for me that he would massage me every night before I went to bed.

God's goodness overwhelmed me. He used Khalid, a Muslim, to comfort and care for me in my hour of need. Khalid had a heart of gold. He often said to me: 'Aunty, if Jesus appeared to me I too would become a Christian.' I longed for him to have such an experience so that together we might praise the Lord. But this was in Jesus' hands, not mine. Although a Muslim, Khalid found the Psalms very inspiring and read them regularly. He found comfort in reading them. Khalid was no stranger to suffering. He had lost two wives in tragic circumstances.

I wished I could have lightened his burden but not being able to wash my own face or dress myself

143

limited whatever I could do. Khalid used to put my dress out for me to put on and even this I could only do with great difficulty. Because of the constant fear of robbery he couldn't hire a servant. With me lying helpless, nothing in the house would have been safe.

We had a surprise visit one day. My younger brother, Alim Shah, his wife and six sons came to visit me. The children, with their natural innocence, said to me, 'Aunty, you don't look different to other people. Father said that Christians are different, but you have two eyes, and two legs like everybody else.' I merely smiled at them. Normality for them meant having the same physical features. Their father had obviously not done a good job at explaining what being a Christian meant. He didn't offer to help me regain my property.

Our only hope to do that was to advertise for help in the newspaper. Within a very short time we received an answer. Two men who claimed that they were detectives said that they would help us if we paid them 2,000 rupees. Khalid, wanting to be the hero, decided to pay them the money. For four months we waited for these detectives to return but we never saw them again. We later learnt that they were imposters. They had hired detective uniforms from a film company. Once again we had been deceived and cheated. When Khalid's brother heard of this he was most upset. He was an inspector in Karachi. 'Why didn't you ask me to help?' he said.

I did not want to embarrass him or cause him any more problems. He had suffered enough as a result of my commitment to Christianity. While I was in England he had married a Mullah's daughter. The Mullah did not know that I was a Christian. When I returned to Pakistan and he learnt of this he said to my nephew; 'I don't want you to have anything to do with any Christian. You like your aunt and you like my daughter. You must choose between them. You cannot have both. You choose which one you will have.' My nephew had replied. 'I cannot ignore my aunt. She is like a mother to me. Religion comes second to me.' Later he and his wife were divorced. He has since remarried and his second wife likes me. They have two children.

I thank God that my nephews and nieces still love and care for me.

Meanwhile, the date for the publication of my book was drawing near and repeated letters came from England asking me for the date of my return. But a change was taking place within me. I was losing my desire to return. I wanted to stay with my family, at least those members of it who did not disown me. I wanted to die in Pakistan here among my own people. As usual I took my burden to Jesus. One afternoon while I was praying in my nephew's house, Jesus spoke to me. 'I will open a door for you in England.'

Back in England, Susan, who had been very sad at my refusal to return, had been praying and fasting. She did this for nine months. Her mother would not let her work with anyone else. She pleaded with me in her letters: 'Please come back. If you don't my life is finished. I don't mind if you are ill. I will look after you.' Her prayers were all infused with this desire for the Lord to bring me back to England.

She prayed like this one night in a prayer meeting. Afterwards, the leader asked her: 'Susan, did you ask Jesus to do something special for you?;' 'Yes,' answered Susan. 'How did you know?' He replied: 'I saw Jesus standing beside you and I heard him say to you, "Daughter, your prayer is heard." Please share with us your prayer request.' But Susan refused saying, 'If my prayer is answered I will tell you.'

A few days later she received a letter from me saying that Jesus had given me permission to return to England. Her mother who seemed to have more confidence than most in the providence of God and, in the power of prayer, had kept the return ticket I had sent when I thought I would not be coming back. In his excitement at the news, her father sent a registered letter but forgot to include the ticket. Out again he had to go and send another registered letter and this time he made sure the ticket was included.

My brother, Alim Shah, heard of my impending return and came to visit me. When he saw the ticket he said to me: 'You know that our brother does not like you because you would not give up your Christianity. It is better for you to go back. You will be happier among Christian people.' The very next day he and my nephew booked a seat for me on Pakistani Airlines. I was scheduled to fly to Karachi. Zenith and Edwin, heart-broken as they were, said goodbye to me at Lahore. I reassured them of my prayers for them.

My nephew Khalid went with me to Karachi. Once again we stayed with Freda's family in Karachi. At 4.00 a.m. the next morning we left for the airport. It was cool and lights were everywhere. The light within me was not burning so bright however. Before we parted Khalid said to me: 'Aunty, I am happy that you lived with me. I learnt so much from you. I shall be lonely after you go. God's love shines through you.' Then it was the turn of my brother. With tears in his eyes he hugged and kissed me. 'Get well and return to us.' 'If it is God's will I will come.' I replied. Then he said, 'Pakistan is your own country. You are always welcome here.' '*My* country,' I said, 'is heaven.'

After I had checked in and gone through we could see each other but could not speak. We just looked at one another. Once again I was in a wheelchair. Khalid had told the stewardess to look after me. Once again I was completely dependent upon others. I had had very little sleep the night before as we had stayed up late into the night talking. The thought of leaving my friends and family weighed heavily upon me. It was a sad farewell.

Once inside the plane, I became quite tearful and wondered if I would ever see my family again. I asked Jesus: 'Lord, what can I do in England in this state? I don't know what sort of relationship you have with me. In 1971 you made me whole and you gave me new life. This year I go to England in a wheelchair even more helpless than I was the first time. Now I have no servants to look after me. Only strangers. How will people receive me? They were so happy to see me when I was healed and well. That had been a sign to them that you had touched me with your marvellous healing power. What is my wheelchair going to witness to? Will not my Christian brothers and sisters say also that you have abandoned me? But it is your will that I go and I am going.'

Jesus answered me. 'This is my will for you. You are mine and I am yours.' With that assurance I closed my eyes. Suddenly, I had a vision of heaven. I saw myself whole and healthy without any deformity. There was no more sorrow, no more pain. Such peace flooded my mind that I forgot my illness and committed all to Jesus.

We arrived at Heathrow at 6.00 pm. Waiting for me was Susan, her brother and Amrar Jeet: they received me with great tenderness. Within one week, I was given a visa for six months. Before I had left Pakistan, my nephew had put 40,000 rupees into my bag. He feared that I would need the money if I was refused entry into England and had to return to Pakistan. He need not have worried. Jesus took care of me.

Chapter 14

Vale of Tears

The vision of heaven I had on the aeroplane was indelibly stamped on my mind but I could not describe it as beautifully as St. John when he says:

> Behold the dwelling of God is with men. He will dwell with them, and they shall be his people, and God himself will be with them. He will wipe away every tear from their eyes and death shall be no more, neither shall there be mourning nor crying nor pain any more, for the former things have passed away. (Revelation 21:3–4)

Until that day, we must walk through this world with its valleys of suffering and its hills of happiness. I have not been spared pain and discomfort in this life but I knew God was my Father and could pray, 'Lord, you have chosen me to live in your presence, even now in this life. What more can I ask? You have said that I am yours and you are mine. What a privilege I have. Use me, just as I am to live for your glory.'

I learnt that physical pain and distress could not separate me from the God who declared to me that He was and is 'Immanuel' – God with us. Instead of my suffering being an obstacle to my faith, I discovered that it could become the means by which and through which God is glorified. I looked to Jesus on the cross and saw him suffering there for the sins of the whole world and bringing glory to God. In my own small way I too could glorify my Father's name.

There was no point in my asking, 'Lord, why did you allow this to happen to me?' Who was I to question the work of almighty God?

In the weeks and months ahead I needed these thoughts to add a new dimension to my faith, to gain this deeper insight. On 28th April 1985, when I arrived in England for the third time, my friends were pleased to see me again and saw my return as the Lord's answer to their prayers. They had held prayer meetings every week, asking the Lord to guide me to return to them. Susan especially was relieved that her nine-month fast had been ended by Jesus himself. At one of these meetings (as I related earlier) the preacher had asked her if she had been praying for something specific. She was too shy to tell him. Then he said to her. 'I have just seen the Lord Jesus standing beside you and putting his hand on your head, and in a very soft voice he was saying to you, "Daughter, don't be disheartened, I have heard your prayer." '

They all welcomed me as if nothing had changed but I knew that life would not be the same for me or for them. I was disabled now and in a wheelchair. They had never seen me like this but it gave them a glimpse of what life had been like for me during the first nineteen years of my life. My healing had been a sign to them that Jesus had touched me with his healing power. How would they react to me now, I wondered.

During the early days after my return I spent most of my time in bed. I had a lot of pain in my leg. Susan's mother, a truly kind Christian lady, felt great compassion for me and massaged me every night before I went to sleep. It was not long before I could begin to walk again. We became very close. One day

I said to her: 'You are my mother now, you must look after me.' She used to call me 'Sister'. She honoured me by replying: 'You are my daughter now.'

This close bond was soon to be severed however. On the morning of 8th August 1985 she was found dead in her bed. I was most distressed by her death but I also rejoiced to see what a beautiful death it was. The day before she died everything had been as normal. We had our prayer meeting and we talked until two in the morning. She said to me before we parted, 'Although you will not be seeing me any more, you will have my daughter with you and together you will work in the Lord's service. Please take care of her because I love her. She is my only daughter and I know I have spoilt her. Please try to understand her.' The next morning she had passed peacefully away into the presence of her Lord whom she had loved so dearly.

Her death left a huge gap in the family. She had been the cementing force in it and now dissensions began to creep in. One of Susan's brothers who lived not far away was married, but his marriage was not a happy one. Consequently, he spent a great deal of time in the family home. This displeased her other brothers and there were frequent arguments between them. One day Timothy came home and found Harry there. He was angry. 'What are you doing here? You come here too often and you stay too long.' Harry meekly replied, 'You know why I am here. My wife has thrown me out.' But Timothy had no sympathy. 'I don't care what kind of relationship you have with your wife, you shouldn't be here. Go back to your wife.' Such were the arguments I had to listen to day after day. At weekends it was worse.

All this reached a climax for me when Harry's anger

turned towards Susan. Susan cried out to her father to help but he seemed powerless and asked Harry to leave but made no effort to see that he did. The fact that Susan had been out of hospital for only a few days, after having had a serious operation and therefore not allowed to do anything, made no impression on him. She had to struggle with him when he began to abuse me and tried to drag me out of bed. He shouted at me: 'You are spoiling our family. You are taking our sister from us. You are a Pakistani. Go back to Pakistan.'

In my stricken condition I could not help myself or Susan. Her father was watching television and the sound drowned the noise of the commotion going on upstairs. In desperation, Susan crawled downstairs and phoned the police. 'Come quickly,' she appealed to them. By now she was shaking violently, both from fear and from weakness as a result of her recent operation.

When the police arrived, they wanted to know what was happening but by this time Harry had disappeared to his own home and all was calm. Nevertheless, they took details from us.

After they left I felt wretched. This was not good for our Christian witness. Jesus' name was being dishonoured. The atmosphere in the home became very unpleasant. Outside, also, the dark clouds were gathering. I soon learnt the meaning of Jesus' words, 'A prophet is not without honour, save in his own country, in his own house and among his own people.'

I knew what it was to be without honour in my own country and in my own home. Now I was to experience what it was like to be without honour among my own kin, my own Asian people. The problems of the domestic life of members of our Asian community flared up again and, almost inevitably, I was drawn in, and got deeper and deeper into trouble. The seeds of discord which had been sown before I had left in 1984 for Pakistan had germinated, and were soon to burst forth into full flower.

One of those involved said angrily to me, 'You are putting ideas into my wife's head. Why don't you mind your own business? Who gives you the right to interfere in our personal affairs?' The bitterness which had taken root in this person's heart began to spread to the rest of our friends, and even those in positions of authority, although openly friendly, were starting to develop a vehement dislike towards me. Yet my only concern was that the name of Jesus Christ should not be brought into disrepute because of our moral behaviour. The Bible was my guide and any advice I gave was always taken from it. The worst thing of all was when those who disagreed with me saw my stroke as a punishment from God.

My father had been concerned about my 'contamination' if I learnt the 'infidel' language. But I was beginning to see that the contamination which occurs in a laxer culture was the more pernicious. For converted Muslims, for whom a strict code of behaviour has always been tied to religion, the problem is not so acute. But for Hindus where the tie between the two is looser, the danger is much more to be feared.

In this tight-knit community in which we were living repercussions of one unpleasant incident tended to be like the ripples caused by a stone dropped in a still pond. Amran Jeet and his family, whose conversion had brought such joy into my ministry for the Lord, found himself in an unbelievable position. His wife's niece, who was divorced from her husband, developed a close and intimate relationship with another key member of our congregation. According to Indian tradition these two should have regarded themselves as brother and sister, but this filial relationship was being violated.

Amrar pleaded with me to try to stop this affair, and when I did try, I only incurred the wrath of the young man. He was preparing to enter the ministry and I did not think that this was a good way to start. He became angry and aggressive. Eventually he secretly married the lady in question in India. Many were hurt over this. His own mother had objected to the relationship but this had had only a temporary effect. Amrar's mother saw the marriage as a sin and stopped going to church. The taboos on marriages are held to be almost sacred. After much prayer the hearts of the whole family were healed and they have since joined another congregation.

But the damage had been done. The Asian congregation was divided. The young man's father was displeased over the divisions created but he sided with his son. He continued to be kind to me, however, and when at the end of October my visa expired, he applied on my behalf for me to·be made a resident. Knowing the opposition of some members of our congregation, he had to keep this a secret. We were all caught up in a difficult situation, in circumstances not always of our own making. The divisions and dissensions precipitated a personal crisis for me. I felt unable to go and worship in the midst of these troubled relationships and I decided to stop attending the Asian church. I was most embarrassed to let my family know what was going on. They believed that I was among fellow believers and I was happy. Whenever visitors came from Pakistan and asked about me

I was very reluctant to meet them. I could not expose what was going on because of the shame of it.

Nevertheless, the Lord continued to use me to witness to his glorious name. I began to visit those Christians who could not attend church. Our fellowship was happy and grew deeper as together we studied the Scriptures. The desire for prayer and for healing did not diminish either. People came with their troubles. 'Please Sister Gulshan, will you pray for . . .' My bedroom became a refuge for the suffering and God used me to bring relief to his people. Many were blessed and healed of their diseases.

One lovely family has continued to be our closest friends. Amir, the six year old son of Shima recognized the power of prayer. 'Sister, Gulshan, I want a brother. Please ask God to give Mummy and Daddy a new baby boy.' I was so moved by this innocent request. His mother, Shima, did not want to have more children, however. 'If I have another baby, it is bound to be a girl. Girls suffer too much in this life. Their mothers suffer too. No, one son is enough for me.'

Even in England where living conditions are so vastly different to those in India, the fear of having daughters still lingers in the hearts and minds of mothers. For first generation immigrants, the tension between the old culture which they left behind and the new which they have adopted continues to trouble and distress them.

I tried to reassure Shima. 'Shima, don't be scared. I will pray for you. When the Lord answers I will tell you.' I prayed daily for one week. One night I could not sleep and was lying on my bed with my eyes closed. At about 3.00 a.m. a picture came suddenly into my mind. Jesus showed me a baby in a plastic bag. He said to me, 'I am giving this boy to Shima.'

On Sunday when the family came to visit me I could hardly wait to give Shima the news. 'You are going to have a son. Don't be afraid to have a baby. It will be a boy.' Soon after she became pregnant and whenever I prayed for her I always prayed, 'Dear Father, look after mother and son.' They often expressed surprise to hear me pray like this. 'Why do you always pray for mother and son? How can you be so sure that it will be a son and not a daughter? When I have dreams, I see myself with two girls.' said Shima. They were looking at my conviction rather than Jesus' promise. He never fails to keep his word. Did he not say that all kinds of signs would accompany those who believed?

There was much rejoicing when Shima had her baby son. Nobody who ever meets them escapes without being told how Imran was born. They even published the news in their parish magazine.

Relationships in the home where I lived unfortunately deteriorated and the domestic squabbles increased. Life there was becoming intolerable. Daily I prayed, 'Lord, you said you would open a door in England for me. Is this the door you promised? The devil is in our midst causing endless difficulties. How can I continue to witness to your name here?' I received no answer.

In 1986 Susan had applied to the local council for a flat, but her application had been rejected. 'You are young and healthy. You can work and earn money to buy one. You are not entitled to a flat. We will put you on the waiting list. If you become eligible and still want one, maybe in 1990 we will consider you again.' With those words another door seemed to be closing.

In 1988 in the midst of all the daily unpleasantness, Susan applied again, this time on my behalf. As a disabled person I was entitled to a council flat. The disturbance with Susan's brothers put the police on our side and when the council phoned them, they were able to describe the conditions under which we were living and recommended us for a flat. Once again, in a crucial time of my life, I found the words in the New Testament to be true.

> We know that in everything God works for good with those who love him, who are called according to his purpose. [Romans 8:28]

A new door was about to open for us. The choice was one which gave cause for rejoicing in God's goodness. Out of eighty flats, Mrs Kelly, the kind social worker assigned to help us, chose a two-bedroomed flat.

It happened like this. Susan was asked to go and have a look at certain flats. While she was waiting at the back of a set of flats she noticed the end one was empty. She took a closer look. 'Please Lord, let it be this one. It seems just right,' she prayed while Mrs. Kelly collected the keys. How delighted she was when this very one was chosen. It was so important for us to have two bedrooms so that we could have visitors and help those in need of prayer and fellowship. In this way I could continue my ministry. Jesus opened the right door for me.

Various attempts had been made to block this opening. Someone rang the council and questioned what they were doing. 'Why are you giving these two people a flat? Gulshan is not even a resident in this country.' Another asked to see the Housing Manager in order to obstruct our path. 'Gulshan is lying. She is only pretending to be ill. She is wealthy and can buy a house of her own.' When one's former friends turn against one, it can be bitter indeed. This particular gentleman used everything he could think of to stop us from getting a place of our own.

Even Susan's family was influenced by him. In fact the family were not pleased to see her move in with me. 'The only way to leave this house,' they announced angrily, 'is by getting married. No reputable girl would dream of leaving her home in this way. Besides your duty is to look after your widowed father. You are bringing disgrace upon our family.'

This was painful to both of us, yet it was Susan's own mother who had given her to be my companion and to work in the Lord's service. Had she not acted according to divine direction? How could this be evil? The situation was misrepresented. Susan's father was not left alone. He had his sons and daughter-in-law. We sought refuge in the fact that we were committed to a greater family than our human one. Jesus himself had said:

> He who loves father and mother more than me is not worthy of me; and he who loves son or daughter more than me is not worthy of me; and he who does not take up his cross and follow me is not worthy of me. He who finds his life will lose it and he who loses his life for my sake will find it. (Matthew 10:37–39)

Those words became a reality for us. We had to experience this particular valley of suffering in order to climb the hill of happiness in being faithful servants of the Lord. His faithfulness strengthened us in our striving to do his will.

Despite the efforts made to thwart his will for us,

we were successful in obtaining the flat which had been promised to us. The Housing Manager, far from being persuaded to change his mind, phoned Susan and asked her to collect the key as soon as possible. At the end of July 1988 we moved into our own premises. When I saw what carpet was on the floor I looked at Susan and she looked at me. We burst out laughing. One day when we had been at the surgery I had said to Susan, 'If we ever have a place of our own, that is the kind of carpet I would like.' Now here it was, a trivial detail but our Lord delights in giving us pleasure in his provisions for us. One week later, to our great amazement, we received a cheque for £1,000 to help us set up our home. Truly He supplies all our needs. Praise his name!

Chapter 15

Home in England

We were now settled in our own home and had to organize our lives as we felt led by the Lord. This was a new beginning for us in more ways than one. We had left the Asian community, with its own church, behind. With their own music and style of worship some members of the Asian church thought themselves superior to other believers. They frowned upon those who joined the parish churches. 'Going there' they said 'is like going to the Hindu Temple. The Christians there are so lukewarm.'

Susan and I shared no such illusions. The questions now facing us was where we should go to worship the Lord on Sundays. 'Which church, Lord?' we prayed fervently as we sought guidance for our lives. We were willing and ready to go wherever He led us. For the first two Sundays we went to St. Aidan's Church in Oxford. On the third Sunday our mini would not start. (It had been out in the courtyard all night as we had no garage then.) We decided to go to the evening service instead.

After the service we introduced ourselves. The preacher asked us, 'Have you tried St. Andrew's? It is nearer to you.' 'No,' we replied, and asked him to visit us sometime. 'Tomorrow I am going to Jersey for a holiday but I will visit you when I return,' he promised.

The very next day the door bell rang very early. 'Who could that be at this time of the morning?'

Susan and I asked each other. Susan opened the door. Standing there was John Samways, vicar of St. Andrew's, and a young man whom he introduced as Rick. 'Did anyone ask you to visit us?' I asked, curious about this unexpected visit.

'No,' he replied. 'After our morning prayers we decided we would visit the Riverside flats and asked the Lord to lead us. We rang the bell of flat number one but that was empty so we rang yours. We were so surprised and pleased when you invited us in, although we have never met. Since these flats were built nearly two years ago, our parish has prayed that we might have Christians living here with whom we could have contact.' We told them a little about ourselves and our search for a church in which to worship our Lord. Before they left we knew where we would go. The place had been shown to us.

Within a month our new home had become the centre of a fellowship group. Every Wednesday a group from St. Andrew's meet here for prayer and Bible study and a few of us share in leading it. Thus my Lord had given me a new sphere of witnessing for him. Our lives at St. Andrew's have been greatly enriched by the fellowship we have found there. When I have needed help with learning English or with answering my correspondence, which by now was growing daily, various members of the congregation have helped me.

My personal ministry has continued. The conversion of Nirmala, now a close and dear friend, is one example of its fruitfulness. She loves to tell her story. Here it is:

'I was born and brought up in Lucknow, India. My family were all Sikhs, but not very strict. When I was twenty, through a friend of his, my father arranged

my marriage to a Christian young man. His family
were only nominal Christians and we went to church
on special occasions only. I lived with his family for
two years and obeyed them in everything, since I
respected all religions. When we came to England
eleven years ago I went with my brother-in-law and
his family to church.

'In 1981 however, two Mormon missionaries came
to visit us in our home. We were very impressed
with their witness and started going to the Mormon
church. Whenever we were absent from church we
were visited by the Mormon members and encouraged to attend regularly.

'All this was soon to change. My husband's aunt
who was on a visit to England from India, and was
staying with us, had heard of Sister Gulshan. She
wanted to hear her before returning to India. I invited
Sister Gulshan to our home but I was too busy to stay
at home and listen. I went to work as usual. One day
when I was out shopping I met Susan and Sister
Gulshan. They invited me to their home on a Wednesday evening when they had their fellowship meeting. After the others had left I talked to her about
my Mormon beliefs. She explained to me that the
Mormons were not orthodox Christians and not an
American form of evangelical Christians. Rather they
are a new religious movement which has a certain
respect for Jesus Christ but which bases its beliefs
more on *The Book of Mormon* than on the Bible and
the Creeds.

'Later I bought a copy of her book *The Torn Veil*
and read her impressive testimony. The truth which
took hold of me most of all was Jesus' promise that
He would return to earth. Before this I had not
thought too deeply for myself about religious truths.

162

I had been inclined to believe what I was told. But now I began to understand things which I never thought I was capable of understanding.

'I realized that only if Jesus were alive now could He return to this earth. Alive, He hears and answers my prayers; alive, He is able to forgive me my sins now as He did the sins of the people in the first century who responded to His message; alive, He can promise me eternal life which begins here and now. I concluded that He must be the Son of God. No one else, however great He had been in the past, could do this for me now in this life. The others are dead; only their messages have remained. Jesus died and rose again and is alive. I can have a personal relationship with Him here and now. He is truly my Saviour in a way the greatest of prophets or teachers could not be. Thus, I, who had blindly followed the leading of others, was overtaken and overwhelmed by these truths. Now I knew in whom I must believe and to whom I must commit my life.

'I developed a great thirst for knowledge of the Bible. My sister-in-law bought me a Bible and I started to read it every day. My understanding of it deepened as I sat at Sister Gulshan's feet and heard her explaining its meaning. I saw her as a teacher sent by God to me. Before I met her I was like a lost sheep but God wanted me to be in His flock and He used Sister Gulshan to bring me in. It was not long before I too started to go to St. Andrew's church to worship my Lord and Saviour Jesus Christ. In April 1990 when I was baptized a new life truly began for me.'

Such personal testimonies as this one from Nirmala gave me great courage to go on with my work. They also gave me much insight into Jesus' words when he said, 'I tell you, there is joy before the angels of heaven over one sinner who repents.'

Five years ago, when my testimony was published, it was considered a 'success' by the publishers. Apart from the many thousands of copies sold in this country it has also been published in seven other languages. I found that more and more people were reading it and trying to make contact with me through my publisher. Invitations kept coming from abroad. In November 1988 I had a visit from a producer and director from Holland who wanted to make a film in Pakistan. I had to refuse all these invitations for one reason: I did not have my passport. It was with the Home Office.

In March 1989 I received a letter from the Home Office telling me in no uncertain terms: 'You are not a resident here. You must return to Pakistan in two weeks' time.' Accompanying the letter was a form with a set of questions – Do you work as an evangelist here? Have you written a book? What is the source of your income? Are you having private treatment or are you receiving it from your General Practitioner? Who looks after you? . . .

Although I had been learning English it was still not good enough to enable me to answer these questions adequately. I needed help. In the old days I would have gone to the pastor of our Asian church. He had developed an expertise in this field and went out of his way to help those who came to him. But I could not ask him now.

As was my usual practice I took the letter and laid it before Jesus. 'Help me Lord to find someone who can answer these questions for me so that I can regain my passport. Lord, you asked me in 1985 in my weakness to come here and I obeyed. Daily I have got better and have witnessed to your goodness. But this door seems to be closing. The Home Office wants me to return to Pakistan. You know all about me. Please show me your will.' With that prayer I left my problem with Jesus.

Susan's birthday was on 18th March and I wanted to celebrate it. Susan protested. 'Please don't bother with my birthday. We have more urgent problems to deal with. If you don't get your passport back and you don't answer those questions you will be sent back to Pakistan. And what will become of all this then?' But I was determined. 'We will celebrate your birthday even if it turns out to be the last.' I invited fifty guests.

Susan was more worried than I realized. That day she prayed continually at work, on the way there and on the way back. I never stopped praying, 'Lord, you know my position better than anyone else. You know me inside and outside. I will not ask anyone else for help. You help me. It all depends on you.' Thus I continued to pray for one whole week. Then one night as I was lying in bed Goa's name came into my mind. Jesus said to me, 'Ask Goa to help.'

Goa was a Hindu. Strange, I thought, that Jesus should use a Hindu to help me.

Next morning I told Susan of the answer to our prayer. Immediately, she phoned her father and asked for Goa's telephone number. Goa was a friend of her father and a retired school teacher. He responded without any hesitation. That very evening while we were having our fellowship meeting he knocked on our door. While we prayed he filled in the form for me and explained to the authorities why I had not replied earlier. John Samways of St. Andrew's wrote a supporting letter to go with my application to become a resident in the United Kingdom.

Two weeks later the postman rang the bell. Susan knew at once what it was. 'It must be the passport,' she said excitedly as she hurried in her dressing gown to open the door. But the postman had dropped a card and went next door. Susan ran after him.

'Oh, there you are,' he said cheerfully. 'I have a registered packet for you.' He handed Susan the long brown envelope. To our great joy it was my passport and a letter telling me to apply to become a resident. In 1990 I would be able to apply for a British passport. This was a miracle to me. The way was now wide open for my ministry. Jesus had kept his promise. I must be faithful in carrying his message wherever he led me.

The very next day I received an invitation to go to Jersey. 'Please come and visit us. Many of our people have read your book and are eager to meet you.' Gladly I accepted this invitation which ushered in a new phase for me. On 10th June 1989 I boarded the ferry. I had never been on a ferry before and the inside of it fascinated me. It was so beautiful and so well furnished. Sleeping on bunk beds in a cabin was certainly a new experience and I was not brave enough to sleep on the upper one. I willingly gave that to Susan.

It was a full ferry that night and we stayed up late, standing by the rail and looking out at the sea. I felt totally relaxed and all my burdens seem lifted from me. The heavens seemed especially beautiful. The words of the hymn came floating into my mind:

> Heaven above is softer blue,
> Earth around is sweeter green,
> Since I know, as now I know,
> He is mine and I am his.

I looked at the water and wondered. Would Jesus walk on the water and come to me as he did when his disciples were in a boat on the sea of Galilee? That would have been wonderful but I knew that he was always with me even when I could not see him.

This trip itself was a sign of that presence. When Jesus said, 'Seek first God's kingdom and His righteousness and all these things shall be yours as well' He certainly meant *all* things. Here we were, with just enough money to live on, well dressed, and travelling because God, through his people in Jersey, had provided for us. I rejoiced that, in heaven, more beautiful experiences awaited us when he Himself will be the continual source of our joy. Not food, not clothes, not travel, but He will be our all, and our souls will be satisfied. I realized how important it was to begin our walk with him now so that at our journey's end, he will be there to greet us.

On Sunday morning around 8.00 a.m. we reached Jersey. Dressed in our Pakistani clothes, we seemed to attract a lot of attention. I was now able to walk without a stick. Someone offered to fetch me a wheelchair but I declined, although I could only walk slowly. Meanwhile all the other passengers walked quickly from the ferry to the gate. Our friends later told us how concerned they were when they could not see us. 'Everyone has gone. Where are they? Have they not come?' they kept asking each other, until at last they spotted two lonely figures making their way at a snail's pace. Their relief showed in their greeting as they embraced and kissed us. I was a little overwhelmed to say the least by this typical French greeting. Such a long way from my days in purdah, I thought!

Robert, who had invited us, was a Port Officer and

was on duty. His friend Julian, a retired Judge, took us to Robert' house, set in beautiful countryside. We were warmly greeted by Robert's wife and children. 'You are our sister in Christ,' they said as they too embraced us. To be welcomed as a sister by complete strangers was a wonderful experience and reinforced my belief that in the new family of God no veil can hide us from each other. When Robert came home our new family was complete.

I was scheduled to address a congregation at 6.30 p.m. in St. John's Church. After a short introduction, Susan and I were called into the pulpit. Here, if anywhere, there should have been a language barrier but there was none. Susan translated for me and the French-speaking congregation understood. Some students who were present asked me if I missed my family. I answered truthfully. 'I do miss them sometimes but I am in the family Jesus has given me.'

And what a family our Jersey brothers and sisters turned out to be! Everyday we were taken by car to see some beauty spot on the island. The sun shone brilliantly, and the weather was excellent. My health improved considerably. I was walking better than I had ever done since my return from Pakistan, in 1985. On the second Sunday I gave my testimony to another congregation and to the women's fellowship group. Everywhere there was such joy in the sharing of our experiences of the goodness of God.

After one glorious week in Jersey, Susan and I returned to Oxford. Other doors began to open for me. Julian, the retired Judge, lived in Brittany and from there came an invitation. August 20th saw us on the coach at 8.00 a.m. as we embarked on our first trip to France. We were greeted by Julian, his wife and two of their friends. This time Julian did not worry when he did not see us with the rest of the passengers. He knew what to expect, and eventually he saw us struggling behind the rest. After a few questions from the French authorities concerning the nature of our visit, we set off for Julian's house.

On the way there, we stopped at his friend's house for tea. Their sixteen-year-old son who had read my book was so delighted. 'When I get to school on Monday I will tell my friends that I have met the lady in *The Torn Veil*,' he said. Three hours later we arrived at Julian's house, a large six-bedroomed house. Susan and I were given separate rooms and, after a good night's sleep, we met Julian's large family of ten children, plus all his grandchildren.

At the 11.00 a.m. service in the Pentecostal church Susan first translated my Urdu into English and then Julian and another Frenchman translated into French. This was the first time I had to be translated twice, but what a patient congregation I had! They sat still and silent, except for the occasional outburst of 'Praise the Lord', for the four-hour service. Perhaps they were used to long services. Pentecostals are never in a hurry to get home.

After the service we were taken to the pastor's home. He lived in a massive house with beautiful mirrors and plants everywhere. He and his wife had no children. The pastor spent most of his time in bed as he was suffering from cancer behind the eyes and had been given only a short time to live. He was scared; he did not want to die. I felt sorry for him. It must have been very difficult for a man in his position to comfort his people with the hope of eternal life and yet be so scared himself of death.

Through Julian I sought to bring comfort to him. I reminded him of Jesus' words in John 14:2–3:

In my Father's house are many rooms; if it were not
so I would have told you. I go to prepare a place for
you. And when I go and prepare a place for you, I
will come again and will take you to myself, that
where I am you may be also.

Then I said to him, 'You have a beautiful house in
heaven waiting for you. Why are you afraid? Your life
is in Jesus' hands, not the doctor's. Medical doctors
only check to see if your body is working well and
give you medication to help if it isn't. Jesus is in
control of your life. He is your true physician. Give
yourself to Him. Don't be afraid. Sometimes Jesus
rejects medical help. Ask him for an answer to your
problem. Look at me. In 1984, on 4th September I
had a stroke in the night and could not get to the
hospital because it was pouring with rain. I was almost
dying and the doctor said that there was not much
hope of recovery. Now here I am walking and getting
better every day. I put everything in Jesus' hands.
He is in charge of my life. You are a pastor and you
preach to people. You must have faith in Jesus Christ
first before you can offer it to others. Open your heart
to Jesus and He will come in. Your cancer is nothing
that His healing power cannot touch if it is his will.
But if it is Jesus' will that you should die, then you
will have a better home in heaven. Do not think so
much of your earthly possessions. If God calls you He
will look after your family. Trust Him. Are you ready?
If you are, then I will pray for you. Take your time.'

Julian explained to him what I was saying. The
pastor said he was ready for prayer. Before we left he
said that he had been delivered from his fear and had
peace of mind. He had cast his burden upon Jesus
who has promised us that when we take his yoke

upon us and learn from him, we will find rest for our souls (Matthew 11:29).

The pastor is alive and well, at the time of writing.

After three days with Julian, we went to St Malo to stay with the nursing manager of the local hospital. His house was on a hillside overlooking the sea. The scenery was magnificent. Although we had to climb seventeen steps to get to his door the panoramic views compensated for our efforts.

Francis, Julian's friend, was a bachelor and lived with his mother and two nieces. The area is noted for good fish and we enjoyed the fish dishes his mother prepared for us. The fast drives along the meandering roads were not so enjoyable although the scenes were spectacular.

From St Malo we went by train to Paris. Lena, an Algerian Muslim lady, had read my book and wanted to meet me. She was handicapped, and Julian had promised that I would visit her when I came to Brittany. Lena's mother and sister had been converted after they read my book nearly three years earlier. When we arrived we found that she had invited several of her Muslim relatives in the hope that they might be influenced by my testimony and message. We had house meetings for three evenings in succession and then two evening meetings in the Pentecostal church of God. Julian translated for me.

Lena and her sister drove us all round Paris, giving us brief glimpses of that historic and interesting city. We could not resist buying a souvenir of the Eiffel Tower to remind us of our first visit to the famous city.

Thus we returned to Oxford, our horizon widened, counting our blessings as we rejoiced in the goodness of our Lord who was giving us an opportunity we would never have had in ordinary circumstances, to see more of his beautiful creation.

In March 1990 a letter was pushed through our letter box. When I opened it I saw that it had been written and posted in Marseilles in December 1989. The postman had mistakenly pushed it through our neighbour's letter box and he was in hospital for two months. Not surprisingly, when Jane my English teacher phoned François he was hurt and disappointed because he thought I had ignored his letter. In it he had pleaded with me. 'Come and visit us. There are many in my congregation who have been inspired by your book to engage in work for our Lord Jesus Christ.'

François, a bachelor, was in charge of a Brethren mission which had four Bible study centres. He was so pleased when I said that I would be very happy to visit him and his congregation in Marseilles. I explained however that I had a busy schedule with many commitments and could not come immediately. More important, I had to seek Jesus' will on the subject since I did not go anywhere without the knowledge that it was His will that I should go. I received several letters from members of His congregation inviting me, but we all agreed to wait upon the Lord for his answer.

That answer came to me and in June 1990. François' congregation sent me two tickets and a sponsored letter. My attempts to get a visa failed twice. The first time I went to the French Embassy, the Lady Ambassador was not satisfied with the contents of the letters I had sent to me and asked for my bank balance. When we returned the following week with Susan's and Jane's bank balances, she again refused to give me a visa, saying that she wanted a statement from my publisher. That same day I went to the French Airlines office and booked two seats with the tickets which François' congregation had sent.

Jane was shocked. 'This is all wrong. You cannot go without a visa. You will be sent back.' When she and her husband took Susan and me to Heathrow Airport on that Saturday morning they were very concerned for us. They expected us to be on the next flight back. Susan too was worried. 'We have no photographs of the people who invited us. What will happen in Marseilles?' Before we left, Jane said to Susan, 'When you arrive in Marseilles, no matter how late it is, ring me. I shall not sleep until I know.'

I was moved by her concern, but I knew in my heart that if there was any problem it would be resolved. I stayed calm and was happy in the French aircraft. I had never been in a small plane before. It was much nicer than the jumbo jet in which I had travelled to and from Pakistan.

On arrival at Marseilles, everyone walked quickly to the passport control centre. Those with British and French passports went through quite easily. By the time Susan and I reached it there was no one there except two policemen and one immigration officer. Susan with her British passport went through without any trouble but I was left standing alone. When I handed in my Pakistani passport the officer expressed surprise that there was no visa stamped in it. 'Where is your visa?' he demanded to know. There was great confusion. Susan tried to explain in English. I spoke Urdu. He only spoke French and kept saying 'No English, please.'

Eventually he managed to find two or three people who spoke English. Outside we could see François and two or three other people holding high our names

– Susan and Sister Gulshan. They looked puzzled and wondered what was happening. After fifteen minutes the officer said to me, 'Follow me.' He led me into his office. The immigration lady understood English and Susan explained to her the reason for our visit and showed her the invitation and letters from François and the others. They called François in. Within a few minutes I was given permission to stay in Marseilles for two weeks. The pattern had repeated itself. My faith in Jesus was not unfounded. Thanks be to God!

François' home and that of his mother and father, who lived next door to him, were on a hill with beautiful scenery all around. Behind the house were hills and mountains. It was Susan's first visit to the mountains and she was thrilled. We were given our own self-contained apartment in the basement. Each morning we were greeted with a kiss by François' mother, whom everyone affectionately called 'Maman'. François' father did most of the driving. He owned three cars and certainly drove them fast! He took us to the various meetings which had been arranged for me and each time there was a prayer for safety on my lips!

In between meetings we were driven round the countryside to enjoy the sight of beautiful fruit trees and flowers in the glorious sunshine. God's creation greeted us in all its splendour. One experience I treasured most. I was able to go up the hills by myself, undisturbed, to spend time praying. I felt truly privileged to do what Jesus himself did nearly two thousand years ago. It was so peaceful there – no noises except the occasional bark of the family's two dogs. The postman only came once a day. The weather was excellent. Everything seemed designed to further my spiritual growth. At night when I walked below the moon and the stars I felt as if I was back in Pakistan in our beautiful garden.

Prayer and Bible study meetings filled our time and many received the Lord Jesus Christ as their Saviour after hearing my testimony for the first time. I was on the radio twice – once on an Arabic station and once on a Roman Catholic station. At the Christian bookshop I spent two hours one day autographing copies of my book. One hundred copies were sold in that short time.

Susan and I returned to England with an open invitation from our friends in Marseilles to visit them again. Some of them have since come to Oxford to see us. A warm and delightful friendship has blossomed between us. It was good to be able to entertain friends in our own home. Whenever we have returned from abroad, I have always felt thankful in my heart to 'be home again'. It may seem strange and may surprise many that England is beginning to feel like home to me. Before I left Pakistan for the third time such feelings seemed remote to me.

I remember how tempted I had been to settle down in Pakistan after my stroke, and rebuild my life with my daughters and son. 'Ma-ji, do you have to go back? Why don't you stay here with us? We will look after you. Here you are with people who love you. No matter how much we disagree with one another, we still love each other. Over there people are suspicious of you. They cannot love you as we do.' So they had argued and pleaded with me.

Such depth of love, and the feeling of security of familiar surroundings, of the sounds of birds and animals evoking cherished memories, the taste of luscious tropical fruit, all conspired to make me think that Pakistan was where I belonged and should stay. The sense of belonging which lies deep within all of us, when securely anchored, creates a peace which can weather many a storm that the tragic winds of life stir up for us. But when that anchor is lifted, one feels at sea and restless. For a while that was how I felt when I left Pakistan for the third time. Now a new anchor was being forged for me, but with the underlying knowledge that I was a pilgrim in this world.

I have reached a point in my life when, as I reflect upon the past twenty years of life, I feel like St. Paul when he said, 'My desire is to depart and be with Christ, for that is far better. But to remain in the flesh is more necessary on your account' (Philippians 1:23–24).

Whether my remaining here in this life is necessary is for my Lord Jesus Christ to decide. My life is where it has always been since he raised me up and told me to witness to his saving power in January 1971 – in his hands. Nineteen years a cripple and twenty years a walking miracle, in many ways and to many places, familiar and unfamiliar, I have taken His message, and my Christian family has grown beyond my expectations. I may never again see many of the people I have met, but I know, and they know, that one day we shall meet on that other shore and in greater light when we shall see Him whom we have loved face to face. Then we shall join that numberless multitude before the throne and shout, 'Salvation belongs to our God who sits upon the throne and to the Lamb.' We shall hear the angels saying as they fall on their faces, worshipping God, 'Blessing and glory, and wisdom, and thanksgiving, and honour, and might, be unto our God for ever and ever. Amen.'

January 1991